BALUCHI GLOSSARY

A Baluchi-English Glossary: Elementary Level

by
Mumtaz Ahmad

Dunwoody Press/Kensington, Maryland
1985

Baluchi Glossary

First Edition 1985
First Impression 1985
Second Impression 2001
Third Impression 2014

All inquiries should be directed to:
Dunwoody Press, 6564 Loisdale Ct., Suite 800
Springfield, VA 22150, USA

ISBN: 0-931745-08-X
Library of Congress Catalog Card Number: 85-70270
Printed and bound in the United States of America

PREFACE

The Baluchi language is spoken by about five million Baluchs living in Pakistan, Iran, Afghanistan and in the south of the Turkmen SSR of the USSR. The majority of the Baluchs, however, live in Pakistan's southern province of Baluchistan, bordering with Iran and Afghanistan. Baluchs are Muslims of Sunni persuasion, the majority of whom live a semi-nomadic life. About 700,000 Baluchs live in Karachi. The Baluchs also constitute an important segment of the Sultanate of Oman in the Persian Gulf.

The origin of the Baluch people as well as their language, has been the subject of considerable speculation among historians and linguists. A Baluch historian, Muhammad Sardar Khan Baloch, in his *History of the Baluch Race and Baluchistan,* has concluded that the Baluch people belong to the Chaldean branch of the Semitic race who migrated from Babylon (Chaldea) in 500 BC and settled in the northern regions of Persia. In the course of time, the Baluchs lost their original Semitic dialect and copiously borrowed from the language of their conquerors, the Achaemenians. Some linguists believe that the Medic branch of the Avestan langauge is the parent of the present Baluchi language. Hence, Baluchi, according to this view, belongs to the Iranian branch of the Aryan sub-family of the Indo-European family of languages. Some other linguists, however, point out that even after pruning all the imported Persian, Indian and Pashto words twined around the classical Baluchi, there yet remains the trunk of a language which is a relic of the ancient Semitic family, both in root and in sound.

Although Baluchi is one of the oldest of living languages, much of its classical literary heritage consists of oral tradition in the form of ballads and folk songs which have been passed from age to age and tribe to tribe through generations of bards and minstrels.

The Baluchi language and literature came to the notice of the outside world in 1830 when an English tourist started research and published his reports. This venture drew the attention of other English scholars; notable among them were Pierce, *A Description of the Mekrani Baluch Dialect* (London, 1877) and Mayer, *Baluch Classics,* (London, 1900) and *English-Biluchi Dictionary* (Lahore, 1909).

The great breakthrough in the development and growth of the Baluchi language and literature came after the creation of Pakistan in 1947 when young educated Baluchs established literary societies, published books and periodicals and tried to revive the creative spirit of their language in competition with Pakistan's other regional languages - Punjabi, Sindhi, and Pashto. In subsequent years, four institutions played a major role in the promotion of the Baluchi language, literature and culture: Radio Pakistan in Quetta -- the capital city of Baluchistan, the Baluchi Academy, Pakistan Television Corporation's Quetta Center, and the Baluchistan University in Quetta. Quetta Radio, which was set up in the early 1950's, provided opportunities for creative expression to a large number of Baluchi intellectuals. During the late 1950's the Federal Government of Pakistan set up the Baluchi

Academy which subsequently became a premier institution for the development of Baluchi language and literature. The Academy has published many books on Baluchi language, literature, culture, and history and has played an important role in encouraging growth of a vernacular press in Baluchistan.

The establishment of the Qüetta Television Center and the Baluchistan University in the late 1960's also played a significant role in reviving the interest in Baluchi language and literature, and in creating a corps of Baluchi intellectuals who take pride in their ethnic and cultural heritage.

The Baluchi language is written in the Arabic script with both nasta'liq and nasx forms. The question of script, however, is far from settled. A meeting of Baluchi intellectuals in Kunchiti (Baluchistan, Pakistan) in January 1982, for example, discussed the issue of script and recommended the adoption of Roman script in view of its simplicity and phonological affinities with the Baluchi language. Other Baluchi intellectuals argued for the continuation of the present Arabic script as they felt that the Roman script would separate Baluchi from other languages of the region.

The present work, *A Baluchi-English Glossary: Elementary Level*, will fill a gap in the field of available Baluchi teaching materials in English. The glossary consists of 2,500 entries of Baluchi words and phrases most frequently used in everyday discourse and in the contemporary Baluchi newspapers, periodicals, and publications of general interest in Pakistan and Iran. It is intended to aid in a more systematic way the teaching and acquisition of vocabulary in beginning and early intermediate-level Baluchi courses.

The entries have been obtained from Ashfaq Ahmad (ed.) *Haft Zubani Lughat* (Seven Languages Dictionary), (Lahore, Markazi Urdu Board, 1978), a monumental work based on word frequency counts of the major regional languages of Pakistan.

The glossary has been designed to be used in several specific ways by both students and teachers:

1) For students at the mid-elementary and early intermediate level it will serve as a mini-dictionary.
2) It will also serve as a vocabulary review list at the end of the elementary-level course.
3) For teachers, it should function as a goal for elementary-level instruction and as a standard for intermediate level instruction.
4) The primary functional utility of the glossary will be, however, in the field of curriculum development. While preparing curriculum/teaching materials in the Baluchi language, this glossary will serve to control the vocabulary used in drills and exercises and help determine which vocabulary items in any text lesson are to be actively acquired. It will thus help in the preparation of graded textbook materials for the elementary text and in deciding which vocabulary items must be glossed in the intermediate text.

Baluchi has six major dialects: (a) the Eastern Hill dialects, (b) the Rakhshani, (c) Saravani, (d) Kechi, (e) Lotuni, and (f) Coastal dialects. (For details, see J.H. Elfenbein, "The Baluchi Language," Royal Asiatic Society Monographs, Vol XXVII, London, 1966). The present work is based on the Rakhshani dialect because of its central location, wide intelligibility, and socio-cultural importance in contemporary Baluchi society. As Elfenbein has noted: "If a choice of a standard dialect were to be made for Baluchi, Rakhshani has stronger claims than any other group to the position." Rakhshani is also a dialect used in radio broadcasting in Pakistan, Afghanistan, Iran and Soviet Turkmenistan.

The glossary uses a four-column format with the Baluchi entry word/phrase in Arabic script, a modified phonemic transcription (see: A Note on Transcription), a grammatical category and an English definition.

I wish to express my gratitude to Mr. John D. Murphy for his help during the compilation of this work. I am also thankful to Prof. M. A. R. Barker whose book, *A Course in Baluchi* (Montreal: Institute of Islamic Studies, McGill University, 1969) was a great help in preparing this glossary. Finally, I am grateful to Mr. Blount Stewart for his willing and efficient cooperation in the preparation of the final draft of the glossary.

M. A.
January 1985
Washington, D.C.

SYSTEM OF TRANSCRIPTION

The system of transcription in this Glossary is essentially phonemic. However, a few modifications have been introduced in order to facilitate an accurate correlation of the transcription with the Baluchi orthography. The Arabic letters having the same sound in Baluchi are therefore represented by different symbols so that the reader can easily relate the phonemic transcription used here with the Arabic/Baluchi script.

/z/ will be represented by z for ز , ẓ for ذ , z̲ for ض , and z̤ for ظ .

/s/ will be represented by s for س , ṣ for ص , and s̤ for ث .

/h/ will be represented by h for ہ , and ḥ for ح .

/t/ will be represented by t for ت , and ṭ for ط .

The following chart shows the Baluchi letter and the transcription symbol used in this work.

ا	a/ə	ذ	ẓ	غ	G
ب	b	ر	r	ف	f
پ	p	ڑ	R	ق	q
ت	t	ز	z	ک	k
ٹ	T	ژ	ž	گ	g
ث	s̤	س	s	ل	l
ج	J	ش	š	م	m
چ	c	ص	ṣ	ن	n
ح	ḥ	ض	z̲	و	w/v
خ	x	ط	ṭ	ہ	h
د	d	ظ	z̤	ے	y/i
ڈ	D	ع	‘		

A NOTE ON VOWELS

ort Vowels

/ə/ a lower-mid central unrounded vowel: the *a* in *above* or the *u* in *but*. Before /h/ followed by a consonant or before /h/ at the end of a word, it is lowered and fronted to the position between the *e* of *set* and the *a* of *cat*.

/ə̃/ the same, nasalized.

/w/ a lower-high back rounded vowel: the *u* of *put* or the *oo* of *took*.

/w̃/ the same, nasalized.

/y/ this symbol has been used in two ways: (1) a voiced alveopalatal continuant: the *y* of *yes* or *you;* and (2) for a lower-high front unrounded vowel: the *i* of *pin* or *sit*. These sounds do not contrast in Urdu; before and after vowels /y/ is interpreted as a consonant; elsewhere this symbol denotes a vowel.

/ỹ/ the same as the second use of /y/ above, but nasalized.

ng Vowels

/a/ a low central unrounded vowel: the *a* of *father*.

/ã/ the same, nasalized.

/e/ a tense mid-front unrounded vowel: the *a* of *fate*, but without the "y-like" diphthongal off glide of the English vowel.

/ẽ/ the same, nasalized.

/i/ a high front unrounded vowel: the *i* of *machine* but without the "y-like" diphthongal off glide of the English vowel.

/ĩ/ the same, nasalized.

/o/ a mid-back rounded vowel: the *o* of *boat* but without the "w-like" diphthongal off glide of the English vowel.

/õ/ the same, nasalized.

/u/ a high-back rounded vowel: the *oo* of *boot* but without the "w-like" diphthongal off glide of the English vowel.

/ũ/ the same, nasalized.

ABBREVIATIONS

adj.	adjective
adv.	adverb
comp. prep.	compound preposition
conj.	conjunction
demon.	demonstrative
interj.	interjection
interrog. adv.	interrogative adverb
interrog. pron.	interrogative pronoun
n.	noun
neg. adv.	negative adverb
pred. adj.	predicate adjective
postpos.	postposition
prep.	preposition
pron.	pronoun
rel. pron.	relative pronoun
v.	verb

BALUCHI GLOSSARY

ا

اَبّا	əbba *n.*	father
اپین	əpin *n.*	opium (also, əfim and əfin)
اثر	əṣ̤ər *n.*	effect, trace, impression, influence
احتن	əḥtyn *n.*	coming, advent, arrival
اَحمک	əhmək *n.*	stupid, foolish
اخیر	əxir *n.*	end, latter portion
اخیری	əxiri *adj.*	last, final
اِدا	yda *adv.*	hither, this way
اداکاری	ədakari *n.*	acting, the acting profession
ادب	ədəb *n.*	respect, regard, etiquette, courtesy
ادب دار	ədəbdar *adj.*	respectful, cultured, cultivated, civilised
ارادہ	yrada *n.*	desire, wish, intention
اُرٛد/ اُڑٛد	wrd/wRd *n.*	army
ارداس	ərdas *n.*	suit, plaint, complaint, seeking aid or justice

ارزاں	ərzã *adj.*	cheap, inexpensive
اَڑس	ərs *n.*	tear (lachrymal)
ارمان	ərman *n.*	desire, longing, wish
اُستاد	wsatd *n.*	teacher, master, expert
اِستار	ystar *n.*	star; luck, fortune
اُستانی	wstani *n.*	lady teacher
اسپیت	əspet *adj.*	white
اشارہ	yšara *n.*	sign, signal, indication, hint, gesture
اُشتر	wštər *n.*	camel
اصلی	əṣli *adj.*	original, genuine, pure, real
افواہ	əfvah *n.*	rumour, gossip
افیسر	əfisər *n.*	officer (also, əfsər)
اقتباس	yqtybas *n.*	quotation, extract
اکیّلا	əkyyla *adj.*	novel, unique, new, strange and marvellous
اَگّ / اَگھ	əgg/əggh *n.*	rate, current price
البت	əlbət *conj.*	although, on the other hand, certainly, but, at the same time, along with this

اُلس	wləs *n.*	public, common people, masses
اَلّم	əlləm *pred. adj.*	compulsory, incumbent, necessary, requisite
الماری	əlmari *n.*	wardrobe, almirah
الّمی	əlləmi *n.*	importance, urgency
الوکا	əloka *adj.*	novel, unique, new, strange
امام	ymam *n.*	"Imam,"a spiritual leader or guide venerated by the Shia sect of Islam; prayer-leader (of a Muslim Congregation)
امّاں	əmmã *n.*	mother *(familiar vocative)*
امان	əman *n.*	safety, security, protection
امانت	əmanət *n.*	deposit, charge, trust, property left in someone's charge
امب	əmb *n.*	mango
اُمید	wmməd *n.*	hope, anticipation, expectation, wish
امیری	əmiri *n.*	prosperity
انڑس	əR̃əs *n.*	tear
اِنسان	ynsan *n.*	man, human being, person
اِنصاف	ynṣaf *n.*	justice, fairness, righteousness

اناگت	ənagət *adj., adv.*	sudden, unexpected; suddenly, unexpectedly
انبار	əmbar *n.*	pile, collection, heap
اندر	əndər *adv.*	in, inside, within
اِنکس	ynkəs *adj.*	this much, so much, this many, so many
انّوں	ənnõ *adv.*	now
انّی	ənni *adv.*	right now, just now
اُنیش	wniš *adj.*	nineteen
اوار بیئغ	əvar bəyyəG *v.*	to meet, get, obtain, join, mix
اواری	əvari *n.*	joining, participating, attending, company, partnership
اوبادگ	aəwbadəg *n.*	offspring, children, issues
اودا	wda *adv.*	thither, that way
اوست	əwst *n.*	hope, anticipation, expectation, wish
اوشتغ	oštəG *n.*	pause, delay, interval, intermission
ایجزی	əyjzi *n.*	humility
ایراد	əyrad *n.*	objection, opposition, criticism, protest
ایمان	iman *n.*	faith, belief, confidence

ایمانداری	imandari *n., adj.*	honesty, trustworthiness, fairness
ایمنی	əymni *n.*	peace, security, safety, tranquility
ایوَک	əyvak *adj., adv.*	alone, only, single

آ

آبات	abat *adj.*	populated, inhabited, settled
آبرو	abru *n.*	prestige, esteem, honor, dignity, respect, chastity
آپ	ap *n.*	water
آپت	apət *n.*	calamity, misfortune, trouble
آپ‌کاری	apkari *n.*	irrigation
آچ	ac *n.*	fire
آدینک	aďik *n.*	mirror
آرام	aram *n.*	rest, ease, comfort
آرت	art *n.*	flour
آڑتی	aRti *n.*	broker, agent (usually a grain merchant)
آزات	azat *adj.*	free, independent
آزاتی	azati *n.*	freedom, independence
آزار	azar *n.*	difficulty, trouble, affliction, adversity, calamity
آزمان	azman *n.*	sky, heavens

آزمانی	azmani *adj.*	heavenly, celestial; sky-colored, blue, azure
آس	as *n.*	fire, flame
آسان	asan *adj.*	easy, simple
آسانی	asani *n.*	ease, simplicity
آستہ	asta *adj., adv.*	slow, gradual, soft, calm, mild; slowly, gradually
آسر	asər *n.*	result, effect, issue, outcome
آسن	asən *n.*	iron
آشوپ	ašop *n.*	revolution, upheaval, change
آغہ	aGa *conj.*	if
آف	af *n.*	water
آفت	afət *n.*	trouble, calamity, adversity, affliction
آف و گواث	afogoaṣ *n.*	weather
آمدن	amədən *n.*	income
آئندگ	ayndəg *adj., adv.*	future, in future
آیغ	ayəG *v.*	to come

باز	baz *adj.*	more, much, too much, too many
بازار	bazar *n.*	market, bazar
بادشاه	badšah *n.*	king
بار	bar *n.*	load, burden, weight
بارگ	barag *adj.*	thin, delicate, fine
باشک	bask *n.*	arm, wing, side; supporter *(metaphorical)*
باقی	baqi *adj.*	rest, remaining, residual
باگ	bag *n.*	garden
بالغ	balyG *n., adj.*	adult, mature
بانگ	bãg *n.*	the call to prayer
بجازی	bəjazi *adj.*	artificial, immitation
بخت	bəxt *n.*	fate, destiny, fortune, lot
بخشیش	bəxšiš *n.*	forgiveness, pardon; tip, gratuity
بد برگ	bədbərg *n.*	protest

بدل	bədəl *n.*	revenge, retaliation, vengeance
بدلی	bədli *n.*	transfer, exchange
بدن	bədən *n.*	body (of a person, animal, etc.)
برات	bərat *n.*	brother
براور	bəravər *pred. adj., adv., adj.*	straight, upright; perfect; favorable, suitable
بُرز	bwrz *adj.*	high, tall, exalted, loud (as a voice)
برگ	bərəg *v.*	to defeat
بُرّگ	bwrrəg *v.*	to cut, sever, carve, bite, cut out
برُوبر	bərobər *adj., adv., comp. prep.*	equal, even, level, straight, uniform, alike, equivalent, adjoining; continually, constantly
برُوبری	brobəri *n.*	equality, parallelism
بُرزاد	bwrzad *adv., comp. prep.*	above, up, upper, over, on
بلا	bəla *n.*	evil spirit, devil; trial, affliction, difficulty, calamity
بلکن	bəlkən *conj.*	perhaps, probably
بندات	bəndat *n.*	basis, foundation
بُن	bwn *n.*	dependence, contingency, reliance

بُنگیج	bwngej *n.*	beginning, commencement, start, inception
بنی آدم	bəniadəm *n.*	man, person
بنیادم گری	bəniadəmgəri *n.*	humanity, humanitarianism, gentility
بودلا	bodla *adj.*	simple, simpleton, naive, plain
بودناکی	budnaki *n.*	progress, advancement, development
بها	bəha *n.*	price, value
بهادر	bəhadwr *n., adj.*	brave, bold
بیان	bəyan *n.*	expression, disclosure, explanation, statement, declaration
بے انصاپی	beinṣapi *n.*	injustice, unfairness
بے تُرس	betwrs *n., adj., adv.*	fearless, bold; without hesitation
بے توار	betəvar *adj., adv.*	silent, quiet
بے دین	bedin *n.*	infidel, unbeliever
بے دینی	bedini *n.*	godlessness, faithlessness
بے زاری	bezari *n.*	dislike, detestation, abhorrence, hatred
بیست و دو	bisto do *adj.*	twenty-two

بیست و سه	bisto səh *adj.*	twenty-three
بیست و هفت	bisto həft *adj.*	twenty-seven
بیست و یک	bisto yək *adj.*	twenty-one
بے سوبی	besəwbi *n.*	failure, lack of success
بے کار	bekar *n., adj., adv.*	useless, futile, invalid, meaningless, unemployed, unemployed person
بیکوب	bekub *n., adj.*	stupid, foolish
بے گناه	begwnah *n., adj., adv.*	sinless, innocent, guiltless; sinless person
بے مناسب	bemwnasyb *adj.*	unsuitable, improper
بے نصیو	benəṣio *adj.*	unsuccessful, failed
بے واکی	bevaki *n.*	helplessness
بے وسی	bevəsi *n.*	helplessness

پاد	pad *n.*	foot
پادار	padar *adj.*	stable, firm, durable
پاد آیگ	pad ayg *v.*	to get up, arise, rise
پاڑه / پاڑو	paRa/ paRo *n.*	quarter of a city or town, ward, neighborhood
پاک	pak *adj.*	pure, clean; innocent
پانزده	panzdah *adj.*	fifteen
پیت	pyt *n.*	father
پٹاٹہ	pətata *n.*	potato
پُٹھّا	pwThTha *adj.*	contradictory, opposite
پجارگ	pəjarag *v.*	to recognise, identify, know
پُجّغ	pwjjaG *v.*	to arrive, reach
پَدّر / پَدّھر	pəddər/ pəddhər *adj.*	prominent, evident, clear, salient, apparent, plain
پرک / فرق	pərk/ fərq *n.*	difference, distinction

پرہیز pərhez *n.* abstention, keeping away from, forbearance, restraint

پریشان pərešan *adj.* worried, upset, troubled, disturbed, anxious, sad

پیڑی PyRi *n.* market, mart

پژم pəžəm *n.* wool

پُسّگ pussag *n.* son

پسل pəsl *n.* crop, harvest; season, time

پسند pəsənd *n., pred. adj.* choice, favorite; pleasing, liking, enjoying

پُشک pwšk *n.* shirt

پشومان pəšoman *adj.* ashamed, repentant, sorry

پکّا pəkka *adj.* solid, permanent, ready, ripe, cooked, matured, substantial

پکار pəkar *n.* need, necessity, requirement

پکّو pəkko *adj.* ripe, ready, matured, solid, substantial, permanent (as a brick or stone house, a paved road, etc.), cooked

پکیر pəkir *n.* beggar, ascetic; carefree

پگار pəgar *n.* salary, wages

پُل	pul *n.*	flower
پنت	pənt *n.*	advice, councel
پند / پندھ	pənd/ pəndh *n.*	distance, space
پنج	pənj *adj.*	five
پنجاه	pənjah *adj.*	fifty
پنجاه و پنج	pənjaho pənj *adj.*	fifty-five
پنجاه و دو	pənjaho do *adj.*	fifty-two
پنجاه و چار	pənjaho car *adj.*	fifty-four
پنجاه و سه	pənjaho səh *adj.*	fifty-three
پنجاه و شش	pənjaho šəš *adj.*	fifty-six
پنجاه و نو	pənjaho nəw *adj.*	fifty-nine
پنجاه و هشت	pənjahvahəšt *adj.*	fifty-eight
پنجاه و هفت	pənjaho həft *adj.*	fifty-seven
پنجاه و یک	panjaho yək *adj.*	fifty-one
پوتاری	potari *n.*	nonsense, foolish talk
پورها	porha *n.*	hard work, labor, effort
پورهاگر	porhagər *adj.*	hardworking, industrious
پوز	pəwz *n.*	mouth, face

پوہ — poh *n., adj.* — wise person, intelligent, wise, sagacious

پوہی — pohi *n.* — wisdom, sagacity, intelligence

پہر — pəhər *n.* — pride, boast

پہسل — pəhsəl *n.* — crop, harvest; season, time; section, chapter (of a book)

پھقیر — pəhqir *n., adj.* — beggar, ascetic; carefree

پُہل — pwhl *n.* — bridge

پھوژ — phəwž *n.* — army

پیتی — piti *n.* — box; luggage

پیدا بیّغ — pəda bəyyəG *n.* — birth

پیر — pir *n.* — spiritual guide; leader of a Sufi order; saint; old

پیروی — pəyrəvi *n.* — following, adherence, observance (of laws, etc.); pursuit

ت

تاپگ	tapəg *v.*	to warm, to heat
تات پچار	tat pəcar *n.*	argument, debate, discussion
تاثیر	taṣir *n.*	effect, impact
تاج	taj *n.*	crown
تاجگ	tajəg *adj.*	fresh
تار	tar *n.*	wire, thread; telegram, telegraph
تاک	tak *n.*	page
تام دار	tamdar *adj.*	delicious, tasty, delightful
تاں	tã *postpos.*	up to, until
تاوان	tavan *n.*	loss, damage, harm, wastage, injury, set back
تاہَرَغ	tahərəG *n.*	pause, delay, interval, intermission
تبا	təba *pred. adj.*	ruined, destroyed, spoiled
تبائی	təbai *n.*	destruction, ruin, devastation
تپ	təp *n.*	fever

تپاس	təpas *n.*	analysis, investigation
تپاک	təpak *n.*	unity, alliance
تخت	təxt *n.*	throne
ترا	təra *pron. (special obj. form)*	you
ترجمان	tərjwman *n.*	interpreter, translator, spokesman
ترسگ	tərsəg *v.*	to fear, be afraid
ترشپ	twršəp *adj.*	bitter
تسلاّ	təsalla *n.*	contentment, satisfaction, confidence, reliance, assurance
تِکّا	tykka *adj.*	sharp, strong, pungent, piquant, hot (spicey)
تکّائ	tykkai *n., adv.*	speed, quickness, hurry; rapidly, quickly
تکڑا	təkRa *adj.*	alert
تمباک	təmbak *n.*	tobacco
تُنّ	tunn *n.*	thirst
تنگ	tə̃g *adj.*	narrow, tight; distressed, straitened, harassed
تنگی	tə̃gi *n.*	narrowness, tightness; distress
تو	təw *pron.*	you *(nonhonorific)*

توار təvar *n.* voice, sound, call

توپک təwpək *n.* gun

تئی təi *pron., adj.* your

تہار təhar *adj.* dark, gloomy

تہارکی təharki *n.* darkness, gloominess

تہل təhəl *adj.* bitter

تہلی təhəli *n.* bitterness, pungency

تہمیات təhmiyat *n.* research, investigation

تیاب tyab *n.* shore, bank, coast, beach

تیار təyar *pred. adj., adj.* ready, prepared; healthy (as a horse, etc.)

تیر tir *n.* arrow

ٹ

ٹوٹا	tota *n.*	piece, part, portion
ٹوک	tok *n.*	thing, matter, word, talk
ٹھپ	Thəpp *n.*	attack, assault

ثبوتی	ṡwbuti *n.*	proof, testimony

ج

جاتو / جادو	jatu/jadu *n.*	magic, enchantment
جانچ	jac *n.*	examination, trial, investigation, scrutiny
جاچگ / جاچغ	jacəg/jacəG *v.*	to examine, test, evaluate
جار	jar *n.*	advertisement, poster, announcement
جاگہ	jagah *n.*	appointment, post, position
جاگیردار	jagirdar *n., adj.*	landowner, landlord
جال	jal *n.*	net, trap
جاسوس	jãsus *n.*	spy
جانشین	janəšin *n.*	successor, heir
جاہل	jahyl *n., adj.*	ignorant, illiterate, uneducated
جائز	jayz *adj.*	permissible, allowable, valid, lawful, legal
جبر	jybər *n.*	force, coercion, compulsion, oppression, predestination
جُپت	jwpt *n.*	connection, attachment

جتا	jita *adj., adv.*	separate, apart, distinct, different, aloof, separately
جتائی	jytai *n.*	separation, partition
جُرمانہ	jwrmana *n.*	fine, penalty
جُړ	jwR *n.*	cloud
جُذا	jwza *pred. adj.*	separated, parted, apart
جُذاجُذا	jwza jwza *pred. adj.*	separated, parted, apart
جُذائی	jwzai *n.*	separation, apartness
جُذّغ	jwzzəG *v.*	to go
جُست	jwst *n.*	question
جمر	jəmər *n.*	cloud
جناور	jənavər *n.*	animal
جنّت	jənnət *n.*	paradise, heaven
جنجال	jənjal *n.*	difficulty, trouble, adversity
جنِک	jinik *n.*	girl
جنگ	jə̃g *n.*	war, battle
جنگل	jə̃gəl *n.*	forest, jungle
جنگلی	jə̃gli *adj.*	wild
جو	jəw *n.*	canal

جواب	jəvab *n.*	answer, reply
جوان	jəvan *n., adj.*	young, young person, youth
جوانی	juani *n.*	morals, ethics, manners, courtesy
جوٹھو	juTho *n., adj.*	lying, false, imitation; liar
جور	jəwr *n.*	fever
جوڑ کنگ	jəwR kənəg *v.*	to make, build, construct
جوزه	joza *n.*	feeling, emotion, sentiment, enthusiasm
جوش ورگ	jošvərəg *v.*	to boil *(intrans.)*
جوُ جوُ	jo jo *n.*	germ, microbe, bacteria
جہاز	jəhaz *n.*	ship, vessel
جُہد	johd *n.*	struggle, striving, effort, endeavour
جُھسّا	jhossa *n.*	enthusiasm, feeling, spirit, excitement, boiling
جھکّغ	jəkkəh *v.*	to bow, bend, incline, lean
جھگڑا کنغ	jhəg Ra kənəG *v.*	to quarrel, dispute, squabble
جہگیر	jəhgir *n.*	land, landed property, real estate
جُہل	jwhl *adj.*	deep, profound

جیڑھ	jiRh *n.*	question, matter, problem
جیگ	jeg *n.*	pocket

چ

چا	ca *n.*	tea
چابک	cabwk *n.*	whip
چاپول	capol *n.*	slap, tap
چات	cat *n.*	(water) well
چادر	cadər *n.*	sheet, bedsheet, veil
چار	car *adj.*	four
چارده	cardəh *adj.*	fourteen
چارِک	caryk *adj.*	one-fourth
چار کِشک	car kyšk *n.*	crossroads, intersection
چاکر	cakər *n.*	servant, employee
چاگرد	cagərd *n.*	environment, surroundings, atmosphere
چالاک	calak *adj.*	cunning, clever, deceitful
چالان	calan *n.*	summons from the police; "ticket"; invoice
چاندی	cãdi *n.*	silver

چانک	cãk *n., adj.*	rent, tear; torn
چانکو	cãku *n.*	knife, clasp-knife
چاول	cavəl *n.*	rice
چاؤنی	cawni *n.*	cantonment, military base
چپّ	cəpp *adj.*	left
چُپ	cwp *adj., adv.*	silent, quiet
چپانٹ	cəpãT *n.*	slap, tap
چپراسی	cəprasi *n.*	attendant, messenger, orderly, office-boy, peon
چپ و چاگرد	cəpocagyrd *adv.*	surrounding, in the environs of, around
چپّی	cəppi *adj., adv.*	upside down, reversed, backwards, wrong (side)
چپّی بوگ	cəppibuəg *v.*	to overturn, turn upside down, turn inside out, reverse, overthrow
چٹّگ / چٹّغ	cəTTəg/ cəTTəG *v.*	to lick, lap
چُٹّگ	cuTTəg *v.*	to escape, get free, go off (as a firecracker), go off, leave, be separated
چِٹّی	cyTTi *n.*	letter, note
چُٹّی	cwTTi *n.*	vacation, holiday, leave

چڈّائیگ	cəDDaə̃g *v.*	to cause to be left, abandoned, to cause to be released
چراگ / چراغ	cyrag/ cyraG *n.*	lamp (of clay, etc.)
چرکی کنغ	cyrkikənəG *v.*	to startle, astonish, astound
چَرو جِر	cərojyr *n.*	wood (for fuel)
چڑھغ	cəRhəG *v.*	to climb, ascend, rise, be lifted, mount, embark
چسّ	cəss *n.*	joke, pleasantry; (literally) taste
چکّاس	cəkkas *n.*	test, trial, ordeal
چکر	cəkər *n.*	circle, orbit, rotation; dizziness, perplexity
چُکّغ	cukkəG *v.*	to kiss
چِل	cil *adj.*	forty
چُلّ	cull *n.*	hearth, stone, fireplace
چِلکغ	cylkəG *v.*	to shine, glow, gleam, flash
چِلّ و پنج	cyllo penj *adj.*	forty-five
چلّ و چار	cyllo car *adj.*	forty-four
چل و دو	cyllo do *adj.*	forty-two

چل و سه	cyllo seh *adj.*	forty-three
چل و شش	cyllo šeš *adj.*	forty-six
چل و نو	cyllo nəw *adj.*	forty-nine
چل و هشت	cyllo hašt *adj.*	forty-eight
چل و هفت	cyllo həft *adj.*	forty-seven
چل و یک	cyllo yək *adj.*	forty-one
چم	cəm *n.*	eye
چماٹ	cəmaT *n.*	light slap, tap
چم دار	cəmmdar *n., adj.*	person in need, pauper, cripple; needy
چنده	cənda *n.*	contribution, donation, subscription
چنگل	cə̃gwl *n.*	grasp, grip, hold
چوٹی	coTi *n.*	peak, top, zenith
چوکی	cəwki *n.*	police post; small stool
چونک	cəw̃k *n.*	crossroads, intersection
چھاپ کنغ	chap kənəG *v.*	to print, stamp (with a design, etc.)
چھاث	chas̤̈ *n.*	spring, fount
چھت	chət *n.*	roof, ceiling

چھتر chəttər *n.* joke, pleasantry

چھتر کنغ chəttər kənəG *v.* to start; to touch, molest, tease, vex, provoke

چھٹغ chuTəG *v.* to escape, get free, go off

چھر chwrr *n.* cave

چھری chwri *n.* knife, table knife

چھرغ chərəG *v.* to graze (cattle, etc.)

چھڑغ chyRəG *v.* to be started (war, a song, music, etc.)

چکھائینغ cəkhkaə̃G *v.* to cause to taste

چِلّ chyll *n.* skin

چھم chhəm *n.* eye

چوکہ choke *conj.* since, whereas

چھیار chear *adj.* clever, alert, cunning

چی ci *n.* thing, object, article

چے cəh *interrog. adv., adj.* What? *(also question-introducing particle)*

چیپک cipwk *n.* chick

چیر بوگ cir buəg *v.* to hide, conceal oneself; to set (sun)

چیڑ	ciR *n.*	anger, rage
چیہانٹ	cihãT *n.*	scream, cry, yell

ح

حاضر	ḥaẕyr *pred. adj.*	present, attendant, in attendance
حاک	ḥak *n.*	dirt, earth, soil, clay
حاکم	ḥakym *n.*	ruler, governor
حال	ḥal *n.*	state, condition, situation, disposition
حالتاک	ḥaltak *n.*	newspaper
حامگ	ḥaməg *adj.*	raw, unripe, immature, nonpermanent, crude
حاویلی	ḥaveli *n.*	large house, mansion
حُبّ	ḥwbb *n.*	love
حِتر	ḥytər *n.*	fear, terror, dread
حد	ḥəd *n.*	limit, boundary, edge, border
حُدا	ḥwda *n.*	God
حِذمت	ḥyzmət *n.*	service
حساوٗ	ḥysao *n.*	account, calculation, estimation, rate; bill; mathematics

خِشت	ḥyšt *n.*	brick
خُشک	ḥwšk *adj.*	dry, dessicated, parched, withered
حقدار	ḥəqdar *n.*	rightful claimant, one having a right
حکم	ḥwkm *n.*	order, command
حکم زوری	ḥwkmzori *n.*	obedience, submission
حکومات	ḥwkumat *n.*	government, state, sovereignty
حملہ	ḥəmla *n.*	attack, assault, invasion
خُونی	ḥuni *n., adj.*	killer, slayer, murderer, assassin; deadly
حیا	ḥəya *n.*	shame, modesty
خیرات	ḥəyrat *n.*	alms, charity
حیران	ḥəyran *adj.*	surprised, astounded, confounded

خ

خاص	xaṣ *adj., adv.*	special, private, particular, choice; specially, particularly
خاص کھاں	xaṣ khã *adv.*	specially, particularly
خاطر	xaṭyr *n.*	mind, heart; service, hospitality, regard, sake; for the sake of, on account of, out of consideration for
خاطر کنغ	xaṭyər kənəG *v.*	to show hospitality, to treat well, receive warmly
خاکی تب	xaki təb *adj., adv.*	modest, unpretentious
خال	xal *n.*	mole
خالق	xalyq *n.*	creator
خاندان	xandan *n.*	extended family, household, lineage, dynasty
خبر کنغ	xəbər kənəG *v.*	to speak, say, utter
ختم	xətm *pred. adj.*	finished, ended, completed, dead
خدمت گار	xydmətgar *n., adj.*	servant, attendant
خراوٗ	xərao *adj.*	bad, spoiled, out of order, rotten, defective

خراوی	xəravi *n.*	fault, defect, bad point, drawback, badness
خرج	xərc *n.*	expense, expenditure, cost, spending
خرج کنغ	xərc kənəG *v.*	to spend
خرید کنغ	xərid kənəG *v.*	to buy, purchase
خزانچی	xəzanci *n.*	treasurer
خزانہ	xəzana *n.*	treasury
خط	xəṭ *n.*	letter; line; handwriting
خلقت	xəlqət *n.*	people, the public, crowd, gathering
خلیج	xəlij *n.*	bay, gulf
خلیفہ	xəlifa *n.*	Caliph, successor, vice-regent, deputy
خمیر	xəmir *n.*	leaven, yeast
خواری	xari *n.*	distress, trouble, wretchedness, degradation
خواہش	xahyš *n.*	desire, wish, will
خوشامد	xwšaməd *n.*	flattery, sycophancy
خوف	xəwf *n.*	fear, terror, dread
خیال	xəyal *n.*	care, caution, safeguarding

خیالی	xəyali *adj.*	imaginary, fanciful

د

دادن	dadən *n.*	alms, charity
دار	dar *n.*	wood, stick
دارغ	darəG *n.*	custody, (police) charge
دارو	daru *n.*	remedy, cure, healing, treatment
داغ	daG *n.*	scar, mark, stain, brand, spot
داغ دیغ	daG deyəG *v.*	to brand (with a hot iron); to fire (a gun, cannon, etc.)
دامن	damən *n.*	skirt, hem of a garment
دان	dan *n.*	grain
دپ / دف	dəp/ dəf *n.*	mouth, face
دپتر	dəptər *n.*	office
دتھاں	dəthã *n.*	tooth
دخل	dəxəl *n.*	entrance, intrusion, concern
دز بندی	dəz bəndi *n.*	request, entreaty, petition
دراج / دراژ	dəraj/ dəraž *adj.*	long, tall

دراژ	dəraž *adj.*	long, wide, vast
درآمد	dəraməd *n.*	stranger, foreigner
دُرآہی	dwrahi *n.*	health
دربار	dərbar *n.*	court (of a ruler)
درجگ	dərjəg *n.*	rank, position, level
درزن	dərzən *adj.*	dozen
درزی	dərzi *n.*	tailor
درس	dərs *n.*	lesson, teaching
دُرستی	dursti *n.*	acquaintance, familiarity, knowledge, experience
درشک	dəršək *n.*	tree
درکنغ	dərkənaG *v.*	to take out, expel, extract, eject
درگاہ	dərgah *n.*	shrine
درگیج / درگیژغ	dərgeyj/dərgežG *n.*	invention, contrivance
درمان	dərman *n.*	medicine, remedy, drug, treatment
دروگ	dərog *n.*	lie, falsehood
دروہ	dərəo *n.*	deceit, delusion, guile, cheating

دروها	dəroha *adj.*	cunning, clever, deceitful
دروگ بند	dərog bənd *n., adj.*	lying, false; liar
دریا	dərya *n.*	river
دڑد	dəRd *n.*	pain; sympathy, pathos
دُز	dwz *n., adj.*	thief
دز دیم	dəzdeym *n.*	ablutions necessary before one performs Islamic prayer
دُزّی	dwzzi *n.*	thief
دُژمن	dwžmən *n., adj.*	enemy
دست	dəst *n.*	hand
دستاں	dəstã *n.*	story, tale
دستور	dəstur *n.*	custom, practice, tradition; constitution
دُعا	dw'a *n.*	prayer, invocation
دعوا	d'ava *n.*	claim, pretension, contention, plaint, law suit
دغا باز	dəGa baz *adj.*	cheat, deceitful, treacherous
دفتر	dəftər *n.*	office; chapter or section of a book
دفن	dəfn *pred. adj.*	buried, interred

دُکھاں	dwkhan *n.*	shop, store
دَگّ	dəgg *n.*	religion
دَگ	dəg *n.*	road, way, path
دَگ	dəg *n.*	habit, practice, custom
دل	dyl *n.*	heart
دلال	dəlal *n.*	broker, agent, pimp
دِلگوش	dylgoš *pred. adj.*	engrossed, absorbed
دلیل	dəlil *n.*	proof, argument, evidence
دماگ	dəmag *n.*	breath, life, moment
دم	dəm *n.*	mind, brain
دُمب	dwmb *n.*	tail
دُنبل	dwnbəl *n.*	skirt, hem of a garment
دنتان	dəntan *n.*	tooth
دُنیا	dwnya *n.*	world
دو	do *adj.*	two
دوازده	doazda *adj.*	dozen
دوت	dot *n.*	smoke, vapour
دو تہ	do təh *adj.*	two times, double

دُود	dud *n.*	custom, practice, tradition
دو ڈوڑ	do DoR *adj.*	two times, double, twice
دُور کنغ	dur kənəG *v.*	to remove, take away, move aside
دوژه	dožəh *n.*	hell
دوست	dost *n.*	friend
دولت	dəwlət *n.*	wealth, riches; state
دوکھا	dokha *n.*	deceit, trick, deception
دوںہو	dõho *n.*	smoke, vapour
ده	dəh *adj.*	ten
دِه	dyh *n.*	village, countryside
دھڑکو	dhəRko *n.*	threat, menace
دَھکّ	dəhkk *n.*	attack, assault
دَھکّ	dəhkk *n.*	rank, position, status
دہکان	dəhkam *n., adj.*	cultivator, farmer, agriculturist
دہکانکار	dəhkankar *n.*	farmer, peasant, agriculturist
دَھکّو	dhəkko *n.*	push, jerk, jolt, shove; loss
دُہمی	dohmi *adj.*	second, other, another, next

دُھند dhwnd *n.* mist, haze, fog

دُھوبی dhobi *n.* washerman

دُھوپ dhup *n.* sunshine, sunlight

دُھوڑ dwhR *n.* dirt, dust

دھیان dhyan *n.* thought, meditation, concentration, attention, heed

دیپانی dipani *n.* defence

دیر der *n.* lateness, tardiness

دیر بیّغ dir beyyəG *v.* to move away, withdraw, get out of the way

دیر کنغ dir kənəG *v.* to remove, take away, move aside

دیس des *n.* country

دیغ deyəG *v.* to give, bestow, grant

دیم dəym *adj.* next, forthcoming, in front, subsequent, following, first, ahead

دیما dima *adj., adv.* straight, direct, upright

دیما dima *adv., comp. prep.* in front, ahead, in front of, ahead of, before

دین din *n.* religion

دینداری dindari *n.* religiousness, piety

ديوال	dival *n.*	wall
ديوان	divan *n.*	court (of a ruler)
ديوانه	divana *n., adj.*	mad, lunatic, crazy, insane, madman
ديوخ	divəx *adj.*	generous

ڈ

ڈاڈا	DaDa *n.*	grandfather (paternal)
ڈاک	Dak *n.*	mail, post
ڈالا	Dala *adj.*	fat, thick, bulky
ڈاہ	Dah *n.*	information
ڈَسّگ	Dəssəg *v.*	to tell, inform, say
ڈَسّغ	dəssəG *v.*	to show, display, exhibit
ڈغار	DyGar *n.*	earth, dirt, dust
ڈُکھ	Dwkh *n.*	pain, ache, suffering, misery, grief
ڈکھیا	Dwkhia *adj.*	difficult, hard, arduous
ڈمب	Dwmb *n.*	tail
ڈنڈ	DənD *n.*	fine, penalty
ڈمبھ	Dəmbh *n.*	scar, mark, stain, brand, spot
ڈوہ	Doh *n.*	sin
ڈوہ دار	Dohdar *n.*	accused person, culprit

ڈیوا	Diva *n.*	lamp (of clay)
ڈیوال	Dival *n.*	wall

ذ

ذات	ẓat *n.*	self, nature, personality; castle
ذبح	ẓəbəh *pred. adj.*	slaughtering, cutting the throat of an animal according to Islamic law
ذرا	ẓəra *n.*	particle, atom
ذرائے	ẓərae *adj., adv.*	just, a little, a bit
ذریعہ	ẓəri‘a *n.*	method, means, way, medium
ذکر	ẓykr *n.*	mention, reference
ذکر کنوخ	ẓykr kənox *n.*	"rememberer", one who praises God
ذمّہ	ẓymma *n.*	responsibility, charge, duty, trust
ذمّہ وار	ẓymməvar *n., adj.*	responsible, answerable, responsible person

ر

راتپار	ratpar *n.*	speed, pace
راج	raj *n.*	rule, government
راجہ	raja *n.*	king, Raja
راحت	rahət *n.*	comfort, ease
راز	raz *n.*	secret
رازق	razyq *n.*	sustainer, Lord, God
راڑ	raR *n.*	rag, small piece of torn cloth
راست	rast *n.*	right, truth
راشنڑ	rašənR *n.*	ration, supplies
راضی	ra<u>z</u>i *pred. adj.*	pleased, satisfied, agreed, consenting, willing
راغب	raGyb *pred. adj.*	inclined toward, disposed toward, desiring
راگ	rag *n.*	tune, melody
راہ	rah *n.*	road, way, path
راہ راست	raherast *n.*	the right path, the correct course of action

رایا raya *n.* advice, counsel, consultation

ربّ rəb *n.* Lord, God, sustainer

ربّال rəbbal *n.* envoy, messenger, emissary

ربّڑ rəbbəR *n.* rubber

ربیع rəbi‘ *n.* spring harvest

رپوٹ rypoT *n.* report

رُتبہ rutba *n.* rank, status, position, level

رحم rəḥm *n.* pity, mercy

رحمت rəḥmət *n.* compassion, mercy, grace

رُخصت rwxṣət *n.* departure, leaving, leave

رُدگ rwdag *v.* to grow

رذ rəz *n.* contradiction, rejection

رزق ryzq *n.* means of subsistence, livlihood, food

رژغ rəžəG *v.* to color, dye, paint

رسید rəsid *n.* receipt

رکّ rəkk *n.* safeguard, protection, safety, guarding

رکّینگ rəkinəg *v.* to save, rescue, cause to escape

رمضان	rəmzan *n.*	Ramazan ("Ramadan"): the ninth month of the Islamic calendar and the month of fasting
رنج	rənj *n.*	sorrow, grief, sadness
رند	rənd *n., adv., comp. prep.*	after, afterwards
رنګ	rə̃g *n.*	color, tint, paint, dye, aspect, appearance
روبرو	rubəru *adv.*	face to face
روژنا	rožna *pred. adj.*	clear, apparent, evident, obvious
روژنائی	rəwžnai *n.*	light, luminescence, brightness, illumination
روش	roš *n.*	sun
روشنائی	rošnai *n.*	light, luminescence, brightness, illumination
روند	rond *n.*	tie, connection, liaison, contact
ره بند	rəhbənd *n.*	principle, basis, rule
ره بندکار	rəhbandkar *n., adj.*	administrative, administerial, executive, administration, executive staff
رهزن	rəhzən *n.*	highwayman, robber
ریز	rez *n.*	rope, string, cord

ریس	ris *n.*	envy
ریک	rik *n.*	desert
ریا رُو	riyaru *n.*	partiality,·taking sides

ز

زا	za *n.*	swearing, abuse, curse, foul language
زال	zal *n.*	wife
زال بول	zal bol *n.*	women, female
زامات/زاماش	zamat/zamaṣ *n.*	son-in-law
زاشت	zãt *n.*	feeling, perception, realisation, sense
زبانی	zəbani *adj., adv.*	verbal, oral, by heart
زبردست	zəbərdəst *adj.*	vigorous, powerful, strict, forceful
ززغ	zəẓəG *n., adj.*	wounded, injured, hurt; wounded person
زر	zər *n.*	gold, wealth, money
زرده	zərda *n.*	a sweet dish of rice and suga
زرزوال	zərzəval *n., adj.*	spend thrift, wasteful person
زرگر	zərgər *n., adj.*	goldsmith
زخم	zəxm *n.*	wound, injury

زُلف	zwlf *n.*	lock, ringlet, tress
زڑد	zəRD *adj.*	yellow, pale
زمانگ	zəmãg *n.*	time, era, period; world
زمانگی	zəmãgi *n., adj.*	old-fashioned, antiquated, orthodox
زمین	zəmin *n.*	ground, earth, land
زمین جُنب	zəminjw̃b *n.*	earthquake; commotion, turmoil
زمین دار	zemindar *n., adj.*	landowner, landlord
زِند	zynd *n.*	breath, life, moment
زنده باد	zyndabad *interj.*	long live...!
زندگ	zəndəg *adj.*	alive, living
زوارخ	zorax *n., adj.*	young, young person, youth
زوال	zəval *n.*	decline, decadence, wane, fall
زوال	zəval *pred. adj.*	wasted, perished, eliminated, vanished
زوان	zəvan *n.*	tongue; language
زور	zor *n.*	force, strength, pressure, exertion, power
زور تور	zortor *n.*	bungling, chicanery, wrangling, deceit; lawlessness

زورگ	zorəg *v.*	to take
زہر	zəhr *n.*	poison
زہر	zəhər *n.*	anger, rage
زہرن	zəhrən *adj.*	annoyed, angry
زہرناک	zəhrnak *adj.*	poisonous
زیات	zyat *adj.*	more, much, too much, too many
زیان	zyan *n.*	loss, damage, harm, wastage, injury
زیبا	zeba *adj.*	pretty, beautiful, handsome
زیمی	zimi *n., adj.*	wounded, injured, hurt; wounded person
زیو	zəyo *n.*	ornament, decoration, embellishment, beauty
زیوناخ	zəyonax *adj.*	pretty, beautiful, handsome

س

سادگ	sadəg *adj.*	simple, plain, blank
سادہ	sada *adj.*	simple, plain, straight forward
ساذ	saẓ *n.*	rope, string
ساڑتھ	saRəth *adj.*	cold, cool
ساڑتھی	saRthi *n.*	cold, coldness; cold season, winter
ساز	saẓ *n.*	apparatus, accouterments, instruments, implements, musical instrument
سازگری	sazgəri *n.*	music
ساسارغ	sasarəG *v.*	to take a short rest, repose
ساعت	sa'ət *n.*	moment, duration
ساکھ	sakh *n.*	prestige, reputation
سال	sal *n.*	year
سال پہ سال	sal pə sal *adj.*	yearly, annual, per year
سامان	saman *n.*	baggage, articles, things, material, paraphernalia

ساہ	sah *n.*	breath, life
ساہی کنغ	sahi kənəG *v.*	to take rest, relax
سبق	səbəq *n.*	lesson, teaching
سپائی / سپاہی	səpai/ səpahi *n.*	soldier, trooper
سِپت	sypət *n.*	quality, attribute, characteristic
ستا / ستاہ	səta/ sətah *n.*	praise, compliment
سِجتا	syjta *n.*	prostration (in prayer)
سحر	səhr *n.*	magic
سحرگو	səḥərgo *n., adj.*	magician
سخت	səxt *adj.*	hard, rigid, strong, severe, intense, violent, extreme, strict
سختی	səxti *n.*	hardness, stiffness, rigidity, strength, violence, intensity, harshness, severity
سُخن	swxən *n.*	speech, eloquence
سخی	səxi *n., adj.*	generous, munificient; generous person
سِدّھا	syddah *adj., adv.*	simple, plain; straightforward, direct, upright
سر	sər *n.*	head, top

سر	sər *n.*	end, extremity, tip; beginning
سُر	swr *n.*	voice, sound, tune, melody, note of the musical scale
سُراغ	swraG *n.*	clue, trace, search
سُراغی	swraGi *n., adj.*	detective, investigator, intelligence agent
سربُر	sərbur *adj.*	superficial, rapid
سرجمی	sərjəmi *n.*	clarification, explanation, elucidation
سرحال	sərḥal *n.*	occurrence, event, happening, incident
سردار	sərdar *n.*	leader, chief
سردی	sərdi *n.*	cold, cold weather
سرزور	sərzor *adj.*	brave, bold, courageous
سرسم	səršəm *n.*	valley, vale
سُرَغ	surəG *n.*	act, action, motion
سرکار	sərkar *n.*	government, my lord, sir (title)
سرگرغ	sərgərəG *v.*	to mend, rectify, improve, correct
سرگوست / سرگو	sərgost/sərgoz *n.*	incident, occurrence, accident
سروغان	səroGan *n.*	ringleader, head of a gang

سری	səri *adj.*	preceding, former, previous, ex-
سریہال	səriyal *adj.*	bold, brave, hero
سڑاغ	səRəG *v.*	to rot, decay, decompose
سڑک	səRək *n.*	road, street, highway
سزا	səza *n.*	punishment
سُست	swst *adj.*	slow, sluggish, lazy
سُستی	swsti *n.*	tardiness, laziness, slowness, slow pace
سطر	səṭər *n.*	line (of writing, etc.)
سکّ	səkk *adj.*	hard, rigid, strong, severe
سِکّہ	sykka *n.*	coin; lead (metal)
سُکّھ	swkhkh *n.*	rest, ease, comfort
سکّھا یںغ	sykhkhaỹG *v.*	to teach, cause to learn
سِکّھغ	sykhkhəG *v.*	to learn
سکّی	səkki *n.*	difficulty, trouble, affliction, adversity, calamity
سلاح	sylaḥ *n.*	weapon, arms
سلام	səlam *n.*	salutation, greeting; hello, goodbye

سندر	səndər *n.*	instrument, weapon
سمارغ	səmarəG *v.*	to put in order, fix, decorate, adorn
سمندر	səmwndər *n.*	sea, ocean
سند	sənəd *n.*	credential, authority, degree, certificate
سنگ	sə̃g *n.*	stone; companionship, company
سنگتی	səngti *n.*	faithfulness, loyalty
سُہنڑا	sohəR̃a *adj.*	pretty, beautiful, handsome
سوادھ	səvadh *n.*	scene, view, sight
سوالی	səvali *n.*	beggar; petitioner
سوَب	səvəb *n.*	reason, cause
سوب	səwb *n.*	victory, conquest
سوج کنگ	soj kənəG *v.*	to ask (a question), inquire
سوداگر	səwdagər *n.*	trader, merchant, businessman
سودائی	səwdai *n., adj.*	insane, mad, lunatic, madman
سوَزْ	səvəz *adj.*	green
سوز	soz *n.*	mourning, grief, lamentation
سوزخات	səwz xat *n.*	vegetable, greenery

سوزی	səwzi *n.*	vegetables
سَوَک	səvək *adj.*	smooth, simple, fluent, easy
سُولی	suli *n.*	hanging, execution
سویث	səveyṣ̈ *adj.*	white
سهث	səhṣ̈ *n.*	jewelry, ornament
سُهر	səwhr *adj.*	red
سی	si *adj.*	thirty
سیاد	siyad *n.*	relative, kinsman
سیادی	siyadi *n.*	connection, relationship, kin
سیاست	syasət *n.*	politics, diplomacy
سیاست زانوخ	syasət zanox *n.*	politician
سیاه	syah *adj.*	black, dark
سیث	siṣ̈ *n.*	profit, benefit, advantage
سیر	səyr *n.*	walk, stroll, pleasure trip
سیر	ser *n.*	"seer," a measure of weighing approximately two pounds
سیک	seyk *n.*	heat, warmth; hot season
سه گیست	səh gist *adj.*	sixty

سیل	səyl *n.*	stroll, walk, walking aimlessly
سینس	səyns *n.*	science
سینغ	sinəG *n.*	breast, chest, bosom
سیه مار	syh mar *n.*	snake
سی و پنج	siopənj *adj.*	thirty-five
سی و چار	siocar *adj.*	thirty-four
سی و دو	siodo *adj.*	thirty-two
سی و سه	siosəh *adj.*	thirty-three
سی و شش	siošəš *adj.*	thirty-six
سی و نو	sionəw *adj.*	thirty-nine
سی و هشت	sivahəšt *adj.*	thirty-eight
سی و هفت	siohəft *adj.*	thirty-seven
سی و یک	sivayək *adj.*	thirty-one

شات	šat *pred. adj.*	**happy, glad, gay**
شاتک	šatək *adj., comp. prep.*	worthy of, suitable
شاخ	šax *n.*	branch, bough
شازه	šaze *n.*	marriage; happiness, pleasure
شاگرڈ	šagəRD *n.*	pupil, student
شال	šal *n.*	shawl
شاله	šala *conj.*	would that...!
شاملی	šamli *pred. adj.*	included in, joined in, admitted into
شان	šan *n.*	magnificence, glory, pomp
شانزده	šanzdəh *adj.*	sixteen
شاواش	šavaš *interj.*	bravo! well done!
شاه	šah *n.*	branch, bough
شاه	šah *n.*	shah, king, ruler
شاہدگ	šahdəg *n.*	highway
شاہر	šahər *n.*	poet

شاہذ	šahyz *n.*	witness
شاہذی	šahyzi *n.*	testimony, evidence, witnessing
شاہی	šahi *adj.*	royal, imperial, kingly
شبہ	šwbəh *n.*	suspicion, doubt
شپ	šəp *n.*	night
شرا	šəra *n.*	claim, contention, plaint, law suit
شراو	šərao *n.*	wine, alcoholic drink
شربت	šərbət *n.*	syrup, sweet drink
شرپ	šərp *n.*	honour, dignity
شرتری	šərtəri *n.*	outdoing, surpassing, excelling
شرکاری	šərkari *n.*	reform, improvement, emendation
شرم	šərm *n.*	shame, modesty, bashfulness, shyness
شرمناک	šərmnak *adj.*	shameful
شرمندگی	šərmyndəgi *n.*	shame, bashfulness, embarrassment
شرو	šuru *n.*	beginning, start, inception
شرّی	šərri *n.*	goodness, excellence

شریخ	šərix *n., pred. adj.*	partner; participating in, joining in, included in
شریعت	šəri'ət *n.*	the "Shiriah," Islamic religious law
شرط	šəRṭ *n.*	condition, stipulation; wager, bet
شُذ	šwz *n.*	hunger, appetite
شزا	šəza *n.*	punishment
شست	šəst *adj.*	sixty
شست و پنج	šəsto pənj *adj.*	sixty-five
شست و چار	šəsto car *adj.*	sixty-four
شست و دو	šəsto do *adj.*	sixty-two
شست و سه	šəsto səh *adj.*	sixty-three
شست و شش	šəsto šəš *adj.*	sixty-six
شست و یک	šəsto yək *adj.*	sixty-one
شش	šəš *adj.*	six
شف	šəf *n.*	night
شکّ	šəkk *n.*	doubt, uncertainty, suspicion
شکّ	šəkk *n.*	comb
شِکار	šykar *n.*	hunting; prey, victim

شکایت	šykayət *n.*	complaint
شُکر	šwkər *n.*	thanks, gratitude
شکست دیغ	šykəstdeyəG *v.*	to defeat
شَکّل	šəkkəl *n.*	sugar
شِکل	šykyl *n.*	face, appearance, image, manner, shape, form, figure, aspect
شِکم	šykəm *n.*	stomach, belly
شگان	šəgan *n.*	taunt, reproach, sarcastic remark
شُما	šwma *pron.*	you
شمب	šəmb *n.*	branch, bough
شموشغ	šəmošəG *v.*	to forget
شموشکار	šəmoškar *pred. adj.*	forgotten
شنبه	šə̃ba *n.*	Saturday
شنگ	šyng *n.*	propogation, circulation, publication
شوزغ	šoẓəG *v.*	to wash
شورش	šoryš *n.*	disturbance, commotion, tumult, agitation
شوشک	šošək *n.*	selling, sale

شوم	šum *n., adj.*	unfortunate, unlucky, unfortunate person
شوقی	šəw̃qi *n., adj.*	person fond of, enthusiast, admirer, fan; fond of
شوق	šəw̃q *n.*	ardent desire, craze, preoccupation
شونگال	šongal *n.*	editorial (note)
شوهاز	šohaz *n.*	sign, signal, indication, clue
شهد	šəhəd *n.*	honey
شهر	šəhr *n.*	city
شه رگ	šəhrəg *n.*	jugular vein
شهری	šəhri *n.*	citizen, urban, civic
شهریت	šəhriət *n.*	citizenship
شهم	šəhəm *n.*	ray, beam
شهید	šəhid *n.*	martyr
شیپگ	šypəg *n.*	sewing
شیخ	šəyx *n.*	sheikh, venerable person, elder
شیر	šəyr *n.*	couplet, verse
شیر	šir *n.*	milk

شیرفروش širfəroš *n.* milk-seller

شیرکن širkən *adj.* sweet

شیشغ šišəG *n.* bottle

شیشه šiša *n.* glass, windowpane, mirror

شیطان šəyṭan *n.* Satan, devil

شیطانی šəyṭani *n.* mischief

شیله šila *n.* cataract, waterfall

ص

صابون	ṣabun *n.*	soap
صاحب	ṣaḥəb *n.*	sir, gentleman
صاف	ṣaf *adj.*	clean, neat
صالح	ṣalyḥ *n., adj.*	virtuous person, pious person; virtuous, pious, righteous
صبر	ṣybr *n.*	patience
صحابی	ṣəḥabi *n.*	companion, friend (used mostly for the friends of the Prophet Muhammad
صبح	ṣəḥəb *n.*	morning, dawn
صحبت	ṣwḥbət *n.*	company, gathering, society, social intercourse
صحت	ṣəḥət *n.*	health
صحو	ṣuḥu *n.*	morning, dawn
صحیح	ṣəḥiḥ *adj.*	right, correct, real, true
صد	ṣəd *adj.*	hundred
صدا	ṣəda *n.*	call, voice, sound

صدّی	ṣəddi *n.*	hundred, century
صرف	ṣərəf *n.*	line, row, array
صرف بندغ	ṣərəf bəndəG *pred. adj.*	arrayed, lined up, arranged
صذقه	ṣəzqa *n.*	alms, charity
صفا	ṣəfa *adj.*	clear, neat, clean
صلاح	ṣəlaḥ *n.*	advice, counsel, consultation
صلاح	ṣəlaḥ *n.*	peace, reconciliation, truce
صندوق	ṣynduq *n.*	box, suitcase
صوبگی	ṣobgi *adj.*	provincial
صوبه	ṣuba *n.*	province
صورت	ṣurət *n.*	appearance, image, manner, shape, form, figure, aspect
صوفی	ṣufi *adj.*	sufi, ascetic, mystic

ضامن	z̲amyn *n.*	security, person responsible
ضامنی	z̲amni *n.*	security, surety, bail, guarantee
ضِد	z̲yd *n.*	contrariness, obstinacy, stubbornness; opposite, antonym
ضرور	z̲əru *adv., pred. adj.*	certainly, necessarily, surely; compulsory, incumbent, necessary
ضرورت	z̲ərurət *n.*	need, necessity, requirement
ضرورت وند	z̲ərurət vənd *adj.*	needy
ضروری شے	z̲əruri šəy *n.*	necessities, requirements, needs, wants
ضلع	z̲yla‘ *n.*	district

ط

طالب	ṭalyb *n.*	student, pupil
طب	ṭyb *n.*	the traditional Indo-Pakistan science of medicine
طرز	ṭərz *n.*	manner, mode, way, kind, type, style; composition (of music)
طریقه	ṭəriqa *n.*	method, manner, way, plan of action
طعنه	ṭ'ana *n.*	taunt, reproach, sarcastic remark
طلا	ṭyla *n.*	gold
طلاق	ṭəlaq *n.*	divorce
طلب	ṭələb *n.*	seeking, desire, call, demand, summoning, sending for
طلو	ṭəlo *n.*	salary, wages
طمع	ṭəm'a *n.*	greed, avarice, cupidity
طویو	ṭəviyo *n.*	physician, doctor

ظ

ظالم	ẓalym *n., adj.*	cruel, tyrannical, heartless; tyrant
ظاہر	ẓahyr *pred. adj.*	clear, apparant, plain, evident
ظلم	ẓwlm *n.*	tyranny, oppression, cruelty

ع

عادت	‘adət *n.*	habit, practice
عاذیز	‘aziz *n.*	distant relative; beloved, dear
عاشق	‘ašyq *n.*	lover
عاقبت	‘aqəbət *n.*	the future, life after death
عالم	‘aləm *n.*	world
عالِم	‘alym *n.*	learned man, scholar, religious scholar
عام	‘am *adj.*	common, ordinary, general, public
عبادت	‘ybadət *n.*	worship, devotion, adoration
عبادت کنوخ	‘ybadət kənox *adj.*	worshiper
عجائب گھر	‘əjaybghər *n.*	museum
عجب	‘əjəb *adj.*	wonderful, marvellous, strange
عجیب	‘əjib *adj.*	strange, extraordinary
عدالت	‘ədalət *n.*	(law) court
عدل	‘ədl *n.*	justice, rectitude

عدل کنوخ	'ədl kənox *n., adj.*	just, judge
عذاب	'əzab *n.*	punishment, torture, torment anguish
عذر	'wzr *n.*	excuse, pretext, alibi
عُرس	'wrs *n.*	death anniversary of a Muslim Saint
عرش	'ərš *n.*	heavens
عرضی	'ərz̲i *n.*	request, petition, written request
عرق	'ərəq *n.*	extract, essence
عِزّت	'yzzət *n.*	honor, dignity, respect
عشا	'yša *n.*	evening prayer
عشق	'yšq *n.*	love, romantic affection
عضبہ	'z̲ba *n.*	part, limb, organ
عِطّر	'əṭṭər *n.*	essence, extract, scent
عقّل	'əqqəl *n.*	intellect, wisdom, sense, mind, reason
عکس	'əks *n.*	picture, portrait, photograph
عکس کار	'əkskar *n.*	painter, photographer
علاج	'ylaj *n.*	remedy, cure, treatment

علم	‘ələm *n.*	banner, flag; standard
عِلم	‘ylm *n.*	knowledge, science, learning
عُمُر	‘wmwr *n.*	age (of a person), life span
عمل	‘əməl *n.*	action, operation, practice, deed, work
عمل داری	‘əməldari *n.*	administration, rule, jurisdiction
عملی	‘əməli *adj.*	practical, operational, working *(adj.)*
عہد	‘əhd *n.*	promise, contract
عہد	‘əhəd *n.*	period, reign, era
عہدہ	‘whda *n.*	post, position, rank, office, status
عہذ	‘əhəz *n.*	marriage contract
عید	‘id *n.*	"Id", the name of the two major Muslim religious celebrations
عینش	‘əynəš *n.*	luxury, sensuality
عینش پسند	‘əynəš pəssənd *n., adj.*	sunsual, debauched, person who lives a life of sensual pleasure
عینک	‘əynək *n.*	glasses, spectacles
عیبو	‘əyo *n.*	fault, defect

غ

غبن	Gəbən *n.*	embezzlement, fraud, misappropriation
غرق	Gərq *pred. adj.*	drowned, sunken, absorbed, engrossed
غرور	Gərur *n.*	pride, boast
غزل	Gəzəl *n.*	a type of poem like sonnet or ode
غُسُل	Gwswl *n.*	bath
غلام	Gwlam *n.*	slave, bondsman
غلط	Gələṭ *adj.*	wrong, mistaken, erroneous
غلطی	Gəlṭi *n.*	misunderstanding
غُلطی	Gulṭi *n.*	error, mistake
غم	Gəm *n.*	sadness, grief, sorrow
غم ناک	Gəmnak *n., adj.*	sad, gloomy, grief-stricken; sad person
غیر اسلامی	Gəyryslami *adj.*	un-Islamic
غیرت	Gəyrət *n.*	honor, esteem, reputation

غیر حاضر	Gəyrḥaẕər *adj.*	absent, not present
غیر سرکاری	Gəyrsərkari *adj.*	unofficial
غیر محرم	Gəyrməḥrəm *n., adj.*	outsider, stranger, one who is not intimate

ف

فاتحہ	fatyḥa *n.*	first chapter of the Holy Quran; prayers recited for a deceased person
فائدہ	fayda *n.*	profit, benefit, advantage, gain
فائدہ وند	fayda vənd *adj.*	profitable, beneficial, advantageous
فتح	fətəḥ *n.*	victory, conquest
فتویٰ	fətva *n.*	religious decree
فخر	fəxr *n.*	pride, boast
فخراگوں	fəxragõ *adj.*	proudly
فرار	fərar *n.*	absconding, escape, running away
فرار بیّغ	fərar beyyəg *v.*	to abscond, escape, run away
فرض	fərz̲ *n.*	duty, obligation; supposition
فرق	fərq *n.*	difference, distinction
فریاد	fəryad *n.*	lamentation, plaint, cry of grief
فریاد کنغ	fəryad kənəG *v.*	to appeal, complain, petition

فریب	fəreb *n.*	deceit, delusion, guile
فساد	fəsad *n.*	disturbance, riot, strife
فضل	fəẕəl *n.*	favor, grace, bounty
فقه	fyqah *n.*	Islamic jurisprudence, Islamic law
فقیر	fəqir *n.*	beggar, ascetic
فکر	fykr *n.*	worry, concern; thought, idea
فلانا	fwlana *adj.*	so and so, such and such, a certain
فلسفه	fəlsəfa *n.*	philosophy
فلسفه زانوخ	fəlsəfa zanox *n.*	philosopher
فلم	fylm *n.*	film, movie
فوت	fəwt *pred. adj.*	dead, deceased
فوټو	foTo *n.*	photo
فوجداری	fəwjdari *n., adj.*	fighting, assault, breach of peace; criminal case
فهم	fəhəm *n.*	intellect, wisdom, sense
فیصله	fəyṣəla *n.*	decision, verdict, judgement
فیض	fəyz *n.*	grace, favor, beneficence, bounty

ق

قابض	qabyz̲ *adj.*	capturing, seizing, taking
قابل	qabyl *adj.*	able, worth, capable, competent
قابو	qabu *n.*	control, custody, grasp, hold
قاتل	qatyl *n., adj.*	killer, slayer, murderer, assassin; deadly
قادر	qadyr *adj.*	the Almighty; powerful, mighty, competent, capable
قاشذ	qašəz *n.*	angel
قاصائی	qaṣai *n.*	butcher
قاضی	qaz̲i *n.*	judge, magistrate; one who administers Islamic religious law
قاعده	qa'yda *n.*	habit, practice, way
قافله	qafyla *n.*	caravan
قالین	qalin *n.*	carpet, rug

قانود — **qanud** *n.* — law, regulation, statute

قانودساز — **qanudsaz** *n., adj.* — lawmaker, lawmaking; lawmaking, legislative

قانودی — **qanudi** *adj.* — legal

قانون زانوخ — **qanun zanox** *n.* — lawyer, pleader, advocate, attorney

قانون گو — **qanungo** *n.* — clerk (of a court)

قاهر — **qahyr** *adj., n.* — cruel, tyrannical, oppressive; tyrant

قائم — **qaym** *pred. adj.* — fixed, firm, established, steadfast

قبا — **qəba** *n.* — (man's) long outer coat, gown

قبر — **qəbər** *n.* — grave

قبضه — **qəbz̲a** *n.* — power, possession, grasp, seizure, holding

قبله — **qybla** *n.* — the direction of the Kaba, the Muslim shrine in Mecca

قبول — **qwbul/ qəbul** *pred. adj.* — accepted, sanctioned, approved, agreed to, consented, acknowledged

قبول کنغ — **qwbul kənəG** *v.* — to accept, consent, agree

قبیله — **qəbila** *n.* — tribe, clan

قدّ — **qədd** *n.* — height, tallness, stature

قدح	qədəḥ *n.*	wine cup
قدر	qədr *n.*	value, amount, appreciation
قدرت	qwdrət *n.*	nature; power, ability, mastery
قدم	qədəm *n.*	step, pace, footstep, foot
قدیم	qədim *adj.*	old, ancient
قدیمی	qədimī *adj., n.*	antiquated, old
قرار	qərar *n., adj., adv.*	slowness, peacefulness, tranquility, ease; slow, peaceful; slowly, peacefully
قرار داد	qərardad *n.*	resolution, motion (in a meeting)
قرآن	qwran *n.*	the Quran, "Koran"
قرآن وان	qwran-van *n., adj.*	Quran reading; devout, pious, God-fearing
قربان	qwrban *pred. adj.*	sacrificed
قربانی	qwrbani *n.*	sacrifice
قرض	qərz *n.*	loan, debt, credit, money borrowed
قرن	qərn *n.*	century; decade
قذرت	qwzrət *n.*	nature; power, strength
قسم	qəsəm *n.*	oath, vow, swearing

قِسم	qysm *n.*	kind, sort, type, category
قِسمت	qysmət *n.*	fate, destiny, fortune, lot
قِصّو	qiṣṣo *n.*	story, tale; event, matter
قصوردار	qəṣurdar *n.*	accused person, culprit; guilty, at fault, blameworthy
قطّار	qəṭṭar *n.*	line, row, queue, series
قُطب	qwṭb *n.*	north
قُطبی	qwṭwbi *adj.*	northern
قُلپ	kwlp *n.*	lock
قلعه	qəl'a *n.*	fort
قلم	qələm *n.*	pen
قمیض	qəmiẕ *n.*	shirt
قند	qənd *n.*	sugar candy
قوّت	qwvvət *n.*	strength, power, force, vigor
قوز	qəwz *adj.*	capturing, seizing, taking
قول	qəwl *n.*	promise, affirmation, word; saying, speech
قِوْله	qyvla *n.*	direction of the Kaba, the great shrine of Mecca which Muslims face while praying

قوم	qəwm *n.*	nation, tribe
قومی	qəwmi *adj.*	national, pertaining to the nation
قومیت	qəwmiət *n.*	nationality
قہار	qəhar *n., adj.*	oppressing, tyrannical; oppressor, tyrant
قہر	qəhr *n., adj.*	violence, turbulence, vehemence; violent, turbulent, tyrannical, oppressive
قہقہہ	qəhqəha *n.*	burst of laughter, guffaw
قہوہ	qəhva *n.*	coffee
قیامت	qyamət *n.*	the Day of Judgement, Day of Resurrection; uproar, commotion, tumult, catastrophe
قید	qəyz *n.*	imprisonment
قیمت	qimət *n.*	price, cost, value

ک

کاټ کوټ	kat kut *n.*	cutting out (clothes), cuts, emendations
کادر	kadyr *adj.*	powerful, mighty, competent; the Almighty
کارتوس	kartus *n.*	cartridge
کارجاه	karjah *n.*	workshop, factory
کارخانه	karxana *n.*	factory
کاردُز	karduz *adj.*	lazy, sluggish, slow
کارډ	kard *n.*	card, postcard
کارکنوخ	karkənox *n.*	worker, volunteer
کاګد	kagəd *n.*	paper
کارګل	kargal *n.*	institute, institution, body, department, organization
کارمرز	karmərz *n.*	use, usage; employment
کار مهتل	kar məhtəl *n.*	strike, shut-down (of a factory)
کاروان	karvan/karvã *n.*	caravan
کاروبار	karobar *n.*	business, trade

کاروکست	karokəst *n.*	trade, occupation, business
کاسه	kasa *n.*	cup
کاغذ	kaGəz *n.*	paper
کافر	kafyr *n.*	infidel, unbeliever
کانود	kanud *n.*	law, statute
کاوه	kava *n.*	coffee
کبا	kəba *n.*	(man's) long outer coat, gown
کبغ	kəbəG *v.*	to fall
کُبل	kwbəl *n.*	lock
کتاب	ktyab *n.*	book
کتاب جاه	kytabjah *n.*	library
کتاب لکهوخ	kytab ləkhox *n.*	caligrapher; writer
کتّار	kəttar *n.*	line, row, series
کُتُب	kwtwb *n.*	north
کُتُبی	kwtwbi *adj.*	northern
کُترغ	kwtrəG *v.*	to cut, trim
کتّ	kətt *n.*	profit, gain, benefit, advantage, interest
کُتّغ	kwTTəG *v.*	to beat, strike, hit, kill

کجا	kwja *interrog. adv.*	where
کچّو	kəccu *adj.*	raw, unripe, immature, non-permanent (as an unpaved road or a building of clay or unbaked brick), crude
کچھّ	kəchch *n.*	duty, obligation
کچہری	kəcəhri *n.*	court of law
کد	kəd *interrog. adv.*	when
کد	kəd *n.*	manure
کدّ	kədd *n.*	height, size
کدلی	kədli *interrog. adv.*	when
کدّہ	kəddə *n.*	wine cup
کرآن	kwran *n.*	the Quran
کرآن وان	kwran-van *n., adj.*	Quran-reading; devout, pious
کرپاس	kyrpas *n.*	raw cotton
کرت	kyrət *n.*	business, trade, occupation
کردے	kərdəy *adj.*	some, any, something, anything, somewhat
کرڑکا	kaRka *n.*	noise, commotion, uproar
کساس	kysas *n.*	estimate, conjecture, guess
کسب	kysyb *n.*	work, task, occupation

کِسِب	kysyb *n.*	deed, act
کَست	kəst *n.*	rivalry, enmity, jealousy
کِشار	kyšar *n.*	cultivation, planting
کِشار	kyšar *n.*	crop, harvest
کِشت	kyšt *n.*	crop, harvest
کَشوک	kəšuk *adj.*	fatal, deadly
کَلاه	kəlah *n.*	cap, hat
کُلپ	kwlp *n.*	lock
کَلیت	kəlit *n.*	key
کُلف	kwlp *n.*	lock
کَلوه	kləw *n.*	message
کَم	kəm *adj., adv.*	few, little (in amount); rarely
کَماش	kəmaš *n.*	president, chairman
کَمُّک	kəmmwk *adj.*	short, curtailed, abridged
کَم لیکه	kəmleka *n.*	minority
کَندوری	kənduri *n.*	table cloth, cloth on which dishes are placed
کَندهی	kəndhi *n.*	shore, bank, coast, beach
کَنَگ	kənəg *v.*	to do (something)

کنگال kəngal *adj.* pauper, poor

کُنڈ kunD *n.* angle, corner

کواؤ kəvao *n.* "kabab," grilled meat patties

کوپگ kəwpəg *v.* shoulder

کور / کھور kor/ khor *n.* blind; blind person

کور kor *n.* river

کوشست košəst *n.* try, attempt, effort, endeavour

کوفغ kofəG *n.* shoulder

کوکار kokar *n.* noise, commotion, uproar

کول kəwl *n.* promise, oath

کوم kəwm *n.* nation, tribe

کومی kəwmi *adj.* national, tribal

کوه koh *n.* mountain, hill

کُوه kuh *n.* (water) well

کھار khar *n.* deed, act

کھار khar *n.* intrusion; concern; influence, jurisdiction

کھاری khari *adj.* useful, efficacious

کُھٹّغ khwTTəG *n.* thorn; fish bone

کھٹّو	khətto *n.*	victory, conquest
کھڈّ	khədd *n.*	cave, ditch
کہذی	kəhzi *interrog. adv.*	when
کہن	kəwhn *adj.*	worn out, old, decayed
کھندغ	khəndəG *n.*	laughter
کہنیں	kohnī *adj., n.*	old-fashioned, antiquated
کھور	khor *n.*	river
کھوڑ	khoR *adj.*	enough, sufficient, a lot of
کیز	kəyz *n.*	imprisonment

گ

گاجر	gajər *n.*	carrot
گاڈو	gaDu *n.*	carriage, cart, train
گاڈی	gaDi *n.*	(railway) train
گاڈی والا	gaDi vala *n.*	person who pulls the cart
گار	gar *adj.*	lost, destroyed
گار	gar *n.*	cave
گار	gar *n.*	intrusion
گارا	gara *n.*	mud
گارہ	gara *n.*	scarcity, deficiency, lack
گاڑی	gaRi *n.*	railway train, cart
گال	gal *n.*	word (vocable), statement, talk
گال	gal *n.*	song, lyric
گالتوار	gal-təvar *n.*	pronunciation
گام	gam *n.*	pace, one and a half feet
گام گوانز	gamgvanz *adj.*	long-paced

گپ	gəpp *n.*	mud
گپّ	gəpp *n.*	conversation, chat, talk
گپ و رپ	gəpp-w-rəpp *n.*	conversation, discussion
گپ و گپتار	gəpp-w-gwptar *n.*	conversation-and-speech, talk, speech
گت و گمان	gət-w-gwman *n.*	guess-and-expectation, expectation
گٹ	gəTT *adj., n.*	busy, engaged, involved, trapped, surrounded; trackless mountain
گٹا	gyTTa *n.*	cheek
گٹگ / کٹھٹھغ	gəTTəg/ kəTh ThəG *v.*	to earn, acquire
گچ	gəcc *n.*	small group, gathering
گچگ	gəccəg *adj.*	grouped, gathered, clumped together
گچین / گشین	gəcin/ gəšin *n.*	election, selection, choice
گراک	gyrak *n.*	customer, buyer
گراں	gərã *adj.*	heavy, weighty
گردگ	gərdəg *v.*	to walk around, wander
گردن	gərdyn *n.*	neck
گردیگ	gərdig *adj.*	circulating, revolving

گِرغ gyrəG *v.* to buy, purchase

گِرغ gyrəG *n.* imprisonment

گرک gərk *pred. adj.* sunk, drowned, absorbed

گِرگ / گِرغ gyrəg/ gyrəG *v.* to buy, purchase

گِرگ / گِرغ gyrəg/ gyrəG *v.* to catch, seize, grab

گرم gərm *adj.* hot, warm

گرمی gərmi *n.* heat, warmth; summer, hot season

گرنچ gərənch *n.* problem, dilemma

گِروخ gyrox *n.* customer

گروخ gyrox *n.* lightening, electricity

گروناک gəronak *adj.* proud, vain, conceited

گریبی gəribi *n.* poverty

گریوی gərivi *n.* poverty; strangeness, state of being a stranger

گریو gəriyo *adj., n.* poor, impoverished; poor person

گڑتی gəRətti *n.* complication, complexity, dilemma, problem, difficulty, confusion, perplexity, worry

گڑد gəRəd *n.* circle, orbit, ring

گڑدغ	gəRdəG *n.*	return, reversion, retreat, arrival back
گڑو	gəRo *n.*	cooking pot, kettle
گڑی	gəRi *n.*	watch, clock
گُذ	guẓ *n.*	cloth
گزّ	gəzz *n.*	yard (measure)
گزر	gəzər *n.*	need, necessity, requirement
گزران زانت	gozrãzãt *n.*	economics
گزرک	gyzyrk *n.*	carrot
گشت	gəšt *n.*	patrol, round, turn, time
گُشغ	gwšəG *v.*	to command, grant, say, do
گُشگ / گُہشغ	gošəg/ gohšəG *v.*	to say, tell; to call something (a name)
گل	gəl *n.*	(political) party, group
گل	gəl *n.*	rejoicing, happiness, celebration
گِلّا	gylla *n.*	backbiting, slandering
گُلام	gwlam *n.*	slave, bondsman
گُلامی	gwlami *n.*	slavery, servitude
گلگ	gələg	herd (of horses)

گلّگ	gəlləg *n.*	wheat
گلو	gəlo *n.*	door
گل و بال	gəl-w-bal *n.*	rejoicing-and-flight; jubilation, great rejoicing
گلّہ	gəlla *n.*	grain, corn
گلہ پان	gələpan *n.*	horse-herd, person who watches over a herd of horses
گلیم	gəlim *n.*	floor
گم	gəm *n.*	sadness, grief, sorrow
گم وار	gəmvar *n., adj.*	sympathiser, friend, one who provides sympathy or solace; sympathising
گنٹگ	gənTəg *n.*	hour
گنج	gənj *n., adj.*	treasure; rich
گنج	gənj *n.*	market, mart
گِندُغ	gyndəG *v.*	to meet, get, obtain, join, mix
گندغ	gyndəG *v.*	to see, behold, observe, look
گندگ	gəndəg *adj.*	dirty, filthy, polluted
گندگ / گندغ	gəndəg/gəndəG *adj., n.*	bad, evil, wicked, unpleasant
گندگی	gəndgi *n.*	dirt, filth
گندوگ / گندغ	gəndok/gəndəG *n.*	meeting, encounter, visit

گندیم gəndim *n.* wheat

گنڈگ gənDəg *v.* to mend (with an awl, as shoes, leather goods, etc.)

گنڈھ gənDəh *n.* problem, dilemma

گنوک gənok *adj., n.* mad, insane, crazy; lunatic

گنوکچادی gənok-cadi *n., adj.* crazy, fool, stupid fellow

گنوکی gənoki *n.* madness, insanity

گوّال gəvval *n.* cowherd

گوانگ goãg *n.* party, feast, invitation, call

گواه gərah *n.* witness

گودو godo *n.* skirt, hem of a garment

گورسی gəwrəsi *n.* caring for, looking after, solicitude

گوش goš *n.* ear

گوش gəwš *n.* breeze

گوشت gošt *n.* meat, flesh

گونَڈ gonəD *adj.* short, curtailed, abridged

گونی goni *n.* annexation; connection, affiliation

گوہر gəwhər *n.* pearl, jewel

گہ	gəh *n.*	jewelry, ornament
گہاتی	gəhati *n.*	prosperity, betterment, welfare
گھاٹائی	ghaTai *n.*	thickness
گُہار	gwhar *n.*	sister
گہتر	gyhter *adj.*	better
گہتری	gəhtri *n.*	greatness, eminence, superiority
گھڑی	GhəRi *n.*	time, moment, occasion; watch
گھوٹغ	ghoTəG *v.*	to rub, scrub
گیست	gist *adj.*	twenty
گیست و پنج	gisto pənj *adj.*	twenty-five
گیست و چار	gisto car *adj.*	twenty-four
گیست و شش	gisto šəš *adj.*	twenty-six
گیست و ہشت	gistva həšt *adj.*	twenty-eight
گیشتر	gəyštər *n.*	majority
گیشتر	geštər *adj.*	extra, supplementary, more, additional, surplus
گیوت	givət *n.*	backbiting, slandering

ل

لاپ	lap *n.*	stomach, belly
لات	lat *adj.*	some, a few, several
لاچار	lacar *adj., n.*	helpless, compelled, constrained; helpless person
لاچاری	lacari *n.*	compulsion, constraint, helplessness; compelling circumstance, factor which compels
لاڈ	laD *n.*	love
لاڈ کنگ	lad kənəg *v.*	to love
لاڈلا	laDula *n.*	beloved, loved one
لاڈو	laDo *n.*	tassel (hung from a camel's saddle)
لاڈی	laDi *n.*	beloved, dear one
لاری	lari *n.*	truck, lorry, bus
لاری ہڈّگ	lari-həDDəg *n.*	bus-station; truck-depot
لاڑا	laRa *n.*	tendency, trend, inclination

لازم	lazym *pred. adj.*	compulsory, incumbent, necessary, requisite
لاش	laš *n.*	corpse, dead body
لاگر	lagər *adj.*	thin, gaunt, ill-fed, weak
لال	lal *n., adj.*	ruby, ruby-like
لال پری	lalpəri *n.*	beautiful maiden, fairy; ruby-fairy
لالچ	laləc *n.*	greed, avarice, cupidity
لام	lam *n.*	war, battle
لامب	lamb *n.*	branch, bough
لامبو	lambo *n.*	flame, blaze
لاہت	lahət *adj.*	some, a few, several
لاہوتی	lahuti *adj.*	divine, divine-inspired
لائخ	layx *adj.*	deserving, suited, worthy
لائک	layk *adj.*	worthy, deserving, suited
لائیکی	layki *n.*	worthiness, capability, ability, fitness, suitability
لباس	lybas *n.*	costume, dress
لبیس	ləbeys *n.*	dress, costume, garment
لپاپگ	lypapəg *n.*	envelope

لتاڑگ	ləttaRəg *v.*	to run over, trample down
لٹّ / لٹھ	ləTT/ləThTh *n.*	staff, stick, cudgel, stave
لُٹّ	luTT *n.*	plunder, pillage, looting
لُٹّگ	luTTəg *v.*	to loot
لُٹّ و پل	luTT-w-pəl *n.*	rapine, pillage, chaos
لج	ləjj *n.*	shame, modesty, bashfulness, shyness
لُچّائی	luccai *n.*	mischief, turmoil, discord
لِچوک	lyccok *pred. adj.*	attached, adhering, imminent, lingering with
لحاظ خاطر	lyḥaz xaṭyr *n.*	regard, consideration, respect, service, hospitality
لحظه	ləḥẓa *n.*	moment, duration, time
لد	ləd *n.*	forest
لڈّ	ləDD *n.*	moving with all one's possessions
لَڈّگ / لڈّغ	ləDDəg/ləDDəG *v.*	to load
لڈّگ	ləDDəg *v.*	to move (one's domicile from one place to another)
لُڈّگ	lwDDəg *v.*	to sway, nod
لڈّی	ləDDi *n.*	bag-and-baggage

لرزگ	lərzəg *v.*	to shiver, tremble
لرزینگ	lərzənəg *v.*	to cause to shiver, tremble
لڑ	ləR *n.*	list, catalogue, table
لُڑ	lwR *n.*	sword
لڑی	ləRi *n.*	chair, string (of pearls, beads); connection, relationship
لس	ləss *adj.*	common, ordinary
لسّہ	ləssa *adj.*	fat and glossy, sleek
لشتی	ləšti *n.*	earrings
لشکر	ləškər *n.*	army, military force
لشکری	ləškəri *n., adj.*	soldier, military man; military
لعب	lə'b *n.*	play, game
لعل	la'l *n., adj.*	ruby; ruby-like
لفافگ	lyfafəg *n.*	envelope
لقب	ləqəb *n.*	title, appellation of honor
لکّ	ləkk *adj.*	hundred thousand
لکّڑ	ləkkəR *n.*	staff, stout stick
لِکّگ	lykkəg *v.*	to write

لکھ	ləkh *adj., adv.*	hundred thousand; countless, innumerable; to an immense extent, as much as possible
لکھت	**lykhkhət** *n.*	writing, composition, passage
لگت / لغث	ləgət/ləGəṣ *n.*	leg
لگڑ	lygyR *adj.*	beggarly, wretched, miserable
لگگ	ləggəg *v.*	to climb, hit, attach, feel, begin
لگوری	ləgori *n.*	cowardice
لمبوگ	**ləmbog** *n.*	flame, blaze
لُنٹ	lwnT *n.*	lip
لُنج	lwnj *adj.*	pitch-dark
لُنکُک	lwnkwk *n.*	finger
لنگ	lyng *n.*	leg
لنگ	ləng *adj., n.*	lame, crippled; cripple
لنگار	ləngar *n.*	plow
لُوت	lut *n.*	desert
لوٹ	ləwT *n.*	demand, claim, desire, want, asking
لوٹائینگ	ləwTənəg *v.*	to cause to be called, invited

لوٹگ	ləwTəg *v.*	to want, desire, ask for, invite
لوٹھ	loTh *n.*	party, feast, invitation
لوچ	luc *adj.*	naked, bare
لذّت	ləzzət *n.*	deliciousness, delight, taste, flavor
لوڈو	lodo *n.*	push, jerk, jolt, shove, loss
لوڑ	loR *n.*	sheaf of grain
لُوڑھ	luRh *n.*	dust storm, windstorm, whirlwind
لوڑینگ	loRənəg *v.*	to roll, mix up, cause to wallow
لوَز	ləvz *n.*	word, vocable
لوَزی	ləvzi *adj.*	literal
لوغ	loG *n.*	house, residential building
لوغی	loGi *n., adj.*	wife; internal, domestic
لوگ	log *n.*	house, home
لوگی	logi *n.*	wife
لولی	loli *n.*	lullaby
لون	ləwn *n.*	kind, color, quality
لونڈ	lonD *adj.*	oval, egg-shaped

لہت	ləht *adj.*	some, a few, several
لیاز	liyaẓ *n.*	regard
لیب	ləyb *n.*	game, play
لیپ	lep *n.*	quilt, coverlet
لیت	ləyt *n.*	skein of thread
لیٹگ	leTəg *v.*	to lie down
لیٹنگ	leTənəg *v.*	to cause to lie down, to lay down
لیک	lik *n.*	line (mark)
لیکھو	likhə *n.*	number, figure
لیمبو	limbo *n., adj.*	lemon; lemon-like; round and plump

م

ما	ma *pron.*	we
مابتّ	mabətt *n.*	love
ماپ	map *pred. adj.*	forgiving, waiving, pardoning
مات	mat *n.*	mother
ماتی	mati *adj.*	maternal, mother-
ماخول	maxul *adj.*	serious, sober, quiet
مادگ	madəg *n., adj.*	female; cow
مادیان	madyan *n.*	mare
مار	mar *n.*	snake
مارگ	marəg *v.*	to check, count, tally
مارگ	marəg *v.*	to recall, review, bring to mind
ماری	mari *n.*	riding camel
ماری سوار	mari-svar *n.*	camel driver
ماڑی	maRi *n.*	building, edifice
مازگ	mazəg *n.*	mind, brain

ماس	mas *n.*	mother
ماسٹر	masTər *n.*	teacher
ماس و پیس	mas-w-pyss *n.*	mother-and-father, parents
ماسی	masi *n.*	maternal aunt
مال	mal *n.*	baggage, articles, things, paraphernalia; wealth, goods
مال	mal *n.*	livestock
مال دار	maldar *n., adj.*	livestock-owning; livestock owner
مال داری	maldari *n.*	herding
مالوم	malum *pred. adj.*	seeming, appearing; knowing, informing
مال ومت	malomət *n.*	property, goods, belonging, stock, riches, wealth and property
مالہ	malə *adv.*	early
مالی	mali *adj.*	of property, relating to property, financial
مالیم داری	malymdari *n.*	awareness, knowledge, information
ماں	mã *prep.*	in, inside, mixed with, among
مان	man *pred. adj.*	in, into

ماندگ	mandəg *adj.*	fatigued, mentally tired, bored, home-sick
مانگ	manəg *v.*	to remain, stay behind
مانینغ	maninəG *v.*	to defeat
ماہ	mah *n., adj.*	month; moon; moon-like
ماہپر	mahpər *n.*	hair (of the head)
ماہپل	mahpəl *n.*	load (of household goods, bedding, etc.)
ماہ رُو	mahru *adj., n.*	moon-faced; beautiful; beautiful one
ماہ دیم	mahdem *adj., n.*	moon-face; fair, beautiful, fair one
ماہیکان	mahy kan *n.*	moonlight
ماہل	mahwl *n., adj.*	beloved
مائی	mai *n.*	Madame, Miss, Misses (term of address or respect used before a woman's name)
ماہی	mahi *n.*	fish
ماہیگری	mahigyri *n.*	fishing
مبارکی	mwbarəkki *n.*	congratulations
مُپت / مُخت	mwpt/mwxt *adj., adv.*	free, gratuitous, gratis; useless, uselessly, in vain
متالو	mytalo *adj.*	misty, mist-covered

مټ	məTT *adj.*	equal, equivalent, matching
مَټ	məTT *n.*	retaliation, revenge
مثال	myṣal *n.*	example, illustration
مُج	mwj *n.*	rainstorm, dust storm
مجلس	məjlys *n.*	meeting, gathering, council
مُچ	mucc *pred. adj.*	supplied, provided, gathered, collected
مُچې	mwcci *n.*	meeting, assembly, gathering
محبت	məhəbbət *n.*	love, affection
محتاژ	mwḥtaž *n., adj.*	person in need, pauper, cripple; needy, indigent
محکم	məwḥkəm *pred. adj.*	firm, fixed, established, steadfast
محکمه	məhkəma *n.*	department
محل	məḥəl *n.*	building, palace
مُخت	mwxt *pred. adj.*	wasted, lost
مختیار	mwxtiyar *n.*	lawyer, attorney
مخلوق	məxluq *n.*	people
مُدّ	mwdd *n.*	crop, harvest; season, time
مُدّ	mwdd *n.*	period, duration, length of time

مُدام	mwdam *adv.*	forever, always
مدان	mədan *adv.*	slowly, gradually, gently
مدت	mədət *n.*	help, aid, assistance
مدت گار	mədədgar *n.*	helper, defender
مدد	mədəd *n.*	help, support
مڈّی	məDDi *n.*	baggage, goods, belongings
مڈّی	məDDi *n.*	treasure, fortune
مڈّی	məDDi *n.*	heritage, inheritance, patrimony
مُراد	mwrad *n.*	goal, aim, objective
مراگا	məraga *n.*	council, committee, commission
مرد / مڑد	mərd/məRd *n.*	man, male
مُردار	mwrdar *n., adj.*	carrion; polluted, evil
مُردگ	mwrdəg *n., adj.*	deceased person; dead
مردم	mərdəm *n.*	people
مردُم گِری	mərdwmgyri *n.*	humanity, humanitarianism, gentility
مرد وار	mərdvar *adj.*	brave, gallant, courageous

مردی	mərdi *n.*	manlihood, heroism, bravery, boldness
مردیګ	mərdig *adj., n.*	manly, stalwart, robust; manliness, bravery
مردین	mərden *n.*	man, male
مرشی	mərši *n., adv.*	today
مرغ	myrəG *pred. adj.*	dead, deceased
مرګ	mərk *n.*	death
مرکب	mərkəb *n.*	horse, steed
مُرګ	mwrg *n.*	bird
مرګ	myrəg *v.*	to die
مرمّت	mərəmmət *n.*	repair, mending
مروچاه	məročã *adv.*	nowadays
مروچي	məroci *adv.*	today
مېړ	myR *n.*	battle, struggle, quarrel
مېړا	myRa *n.*	battle, struggle
مړا دار	məRadar *adj.*	courageous
مړا داری	məRadari *n.*	courage
مړدم	məRdəm *n.*	man

مڑگ	myRəg *v.*	to fight
مُزّ	mwzz *n.*	wages, pay, fare; fee
مزار	məzar *n.*	tiger
مزت‌گار	məzətgar *n., adj.*	helper, supporter
مُزد	mwzd *n.*	wages, remuneration, pay, compensation, fare, fee
مِزّل	myzzyl *n.*	stage of journey (approximately 32 miles)
مِزّل	myzzəl *n.*	distance, space
مزن	məzən *adj., n.*	great, high, exalted; great person
مزن	məzən *adj.*	broad, vast, spacious, wide
مزنی	məzni *n.*	value, appreciation; amount, honor
مزنی	məzni *n.*	virtue, greatness, eminence
مزور	məzur *n.*	manual labor, worker
مزیدار	məzedar *adj.*	delicious
مُژ	mwž *n.*	mist, haze, fog
مِس	mys *n.*	urine
مُساپر	mwsapyr *n.*	traveller
مسافر	mwsafyr *n., adj.*	traveller; travelling

مسافری	mwsafri *n.*	journey, travel
مثال	mysal *n.*	example
مست	məst *adj.*	intoxicated, enraptured, ecstatic
مستاگ	mystag *n.*	reward (for bringing good news)
مستری	məstri *n.*	superiority, eminence, greatness
مستِری	məstyri *n.2*	value, appreciation, honor
مستغ	məstəG *n.*	curds, yoghurt
مسک	mysk *n., adj.*	musk; musk-scented
مسلمان	mwsləlman *n., adj.*	Muslim
مسیت	məsit *n.*	mosque
مُشت	mwšt *n.*	instalment
مُشک	mwšk *n.*	mouse, rat
مشکل	mwškyl *n., adj.*	difficulty, hardship, problem; difficult, hard
مشگ	mwšəg *v.*	to rub, polish
میشین	myšin *n.*	machine
مضمون	məzmun *n.*	writing, composition, text, passage, essay, article

مطلو	mətlo *n.*	meaning, concern, aim, object, need
معاف	m'af *pred. adj.*	forgiving, pardoning, waiving
معتبر	m'otəbər *n.*	influential person
معصوم	ma'ṣum *adj.,n.*	innocent, guiltless; innocent person
معقول	m'aqul *adj.*	quiet, serious, sober
معلوم	m'alum *pred. adj.*	knowing, appearing, informing, seeing
مغز	məGəz *n.*	mind, brain
مكان	məkan *n.*	house, residential building
مكر	məkr *n.*	cunning, deceit, cheating, pretense
مكن	məkən *pred. adj.*	forbidden, prohibited
مگه	məgə *conj.*	but
مُلّا	mwlla *n.*	Mulla, Muslim religious functionary
ملام	məlam *n.*	bribe
ملام	malam *n.*	accusation, allegation, indictment, blame
ملامی	məlami *n.*	accused person, culprit
ملپد	məlpəd *n.*	meadow

مِلَغ	myləG *v.*	to meet, get, obtain, join, mix
مِلک	mylk *n.*	estate, property, possession
مُلک	mwlk *n.*	country, state, realm, land
مَلّگ	məlləg *v.*	to move smoothly, flow (as water)
مَلّگی	məlləgi *adj.*	smooth-moving, flowing, graceful
ملنڈ	mələnD *n.*	joke
ملنگ	mələng *n.*	holy man, ascetic, faqir
ملور	məlor *adj., n.*	sad, gloomy, grief-stricken; sad person
من	mən *pron.*	I
من	mən *prep.*	in, inside, mixed into, intermingled in, among
من	mən *n.*	maund, a measure weighing approximately eighty pounds
منّ	mənn *n.*	recognition (of someone's qualities), appreciation, avowal, admission (of a crime, fault, etc.)
مناسف	munasyf *adj.*	suitable, capable
مِنّت	mynnətt *n.*	kindness, benevolence, goodness, favour, obligation, entreaty, supplication, urging

منٹ	mynəTT *n.*	minute
منج	mənj *n.*	open area
مندر	məndər *adj.*	short (of persons)
مندیل	məndil *n.*	turban
منڈ	mwnd *n., adj.*	cut off, severed; lame, crippled, handicapped; cripple, handicap
منزور	mənzur *pred. adj.*	approved, accepted
منزل	mənzyl *n.*	trip, journey, stages of a journey
منسب	mənsəb *n.*	post, office
منسبدار	mənsəbdar *n.*	official, functionary
منشا	mənša *n.*	desire, will
منّشت	mənnyšt *n.*	vow, offering, sacrifice
مُنشی	mwnši *n.*	clerk
منصب	mənṣəb *n.*	class, degree, level, rank, post, office
منصبدار	mənṣəbdar *n.*	official, functionary
منصف	mwnṣyf *n., adj.*	just, judicious; just person
منظور	mənẓur *pred. adj.*	accepted, consented, acknowledged

منظور کنغ	mənẓur kənəG *v.*	to accept, consent, agree
منّغ	mənnəG *pred. adj.*	accepted, believed, consented
منّگ	mənnəg *v.*	to obey, approve, agree
منّگ/منّغ	mənnəg/mənnəG *v.*	to believe, obey, accept
منّوخ	mənnox *n., adj.*	devoted, attached
منّوخ	mənnox *pred. adj.*	agreeing, accepting, believing confessing
موارک	mwarək *adj.*	blessed, auspicious
موارک باش	mwarək baṣ *n.*	congratulations
موبّت	mobətt *n.*	love, affection
موتبر	motəbər *n.*	influential person
موٹل	moTəl *n.*	car, automobile
موج دار	məwjdar *adj.*	passionate, yearning
مور دانگ	mordanəg *n.*	finger
مورنیک	morink *n.*	ant
موسم	məwsəm *n.*	season, weather,climate
موکل	mokəl *n.*	farewell, leaving
مولوی	məwləvi *n.*	Maulvi, Muslim religious functionary
مه	mə *prep.*	in, inside, mixed into

مہاری	məhari *n.*	riding camel
مہاری سوار	məhari svar *n.*	camel driver
مہپر	məhpər *n.*	hair
مہپل	məhpəl *n.*	load, burden
مہتر	məhtər *adj., n.*	chief, noble; prestigious person
مہتلی	mehtali *n.*	postponement, delaying
مہدی	məhdi *n.*	Mahdi, the religious guide who, according to the . Islamic belief, will be sent by God to guide mankind at the end of time
مہر	məhr *n.*	love, affection, grace
مہربان	məhrban *adj.*	kind, affectionate
مہربانی	məhrbani *n.*	kindness
مہروان	myhrvan *n., adj.*	kind person; kind, friendly, gracious
مہروانی	məhrvani *n.*	kindness, graciousness
مہریگ	məhreg *adj., n.*	dear, beloved
مہذب/مہذو	məhzəb/məhzəw *n.*	religion
مہل	məhl *n.*	time, period, age
مہلوک	məhluk *n.*	people, folks

میہمان	myhman *n.*	guest, visitor
میہمان دار	məhmandar *n., adj.*	host
میہمان داری	məhmandari *n.*	hospitality
میا	mia *n.*	holy man, faqir, ascetic
میاذ	miyaẓ *n.*	period, term, time, interval
میار	məyar *n.*	dishonor, blemish upon one's honor; sum paid in compensation for a blemish upon one's honor
میاں	miã *n.*	holy man, faqir, ascetic
میان	myan *n., adj.*	middle, waist; middle (adj.), mid
میّت	məyyət *n.*	corpse, dead body
میچ	mej *n.*	table
میذان	meyzan *n.*	field, open field, ground, playground
میدان	məydan *n.*	field, ground, plain, playground
میر	mer *n.*	grace, beneficience, love
میر	mir *n., adj.*	noble, person belonging to a chief's family
میراث	mirat *n.*	inheritance

میربان	merban *adj.*	kind, affectionate
میربانی	merbani *n.*	kindness
میریگ	mireg *adj., n.*	beloved, dear
میڑه	miRa *n.*	crowd, throng, mob, concourse
میڑو	meRəv *n.*	assembly, parliament
میڑینگ	meRənəg *v.*	to cause to fight
میز	mez *n.*	table
میسینگ	misenəg *v.*	to wet, soak, drench
میش	meš *n.*	sheep
میکمگ	məykəməg *n.*	department
میل	məyl *n.*	inclination, tendency, desire
میل	mil *n.*	mile
میمان	meman *n.*	guest
میمان دار	memandar *n., adj.*	host
میمان داری	memandari *n.*	hospitality
مینگ	mənəg *v.*	to wet, soak, drench
میهتر	mehtər *adj., n.*	noble, chief, prestigious person
میهریگ	mehrig *adj., n.*	beloved, dear

ن

نا امپاد	naəmpad *adj.*	ephemeral, impermanent
نا اُمیتی / نا اُمیدی	nawmiti/nawmidi *n.*	disappointment, despair
نا انجاری	naənjari *n.*	disagreement, dissension
نا اومیتی	naometi *n.*	hopelessness, despair
نا اهل	naəhl *adj., n.*	incapable, unworthy, unfit; unworthy person
ناپګ	napəg *n.*	navel
ناپید	napəyd *adj.*	unique, strange, unparallelled
ناپیدی	napəydi *n.*	dearth
ناتپاکی	natpaki *n.*	disagreement, discord, difference, opposition, variance, disunity
ناتمام	natəman *adj.*	incomplete, unfinished
ناتوام	natvam *adj.*	half-done, incomplete
ناجوړ	najoR *adj., n.*	sick, ill; sick person, patient
ناجوړی	najoRi *n.*	sickness, illness, disease
ناچ	nac *n.*	dance

ناحق   naḥəq *adj., adv.*   useless, profitless, to no avail, in vain, for nothing

نادار   nadar *adj., n.*   poor, destitute

نادر   nadyr *adj.*   wonderful, unusual, rare

نادراه   nadwrah *adj.*   sick, ill

نادینگ   nadenəg *v.*   to cause to sit, seat (someone)

نازان   naẓan *adj.*   naive, foolish, ignorant

نازانت   naẓant *adj.*   foolish, ignorant

نازانی   naẓani *n.*   naiveté, foolishness, ignorance

ناراضی   naraẕi *n.*   anger, rage

نارضا   naraẕa *adj.*   annoyed, angry

نارنج   narynj *n.*   orange (fruit)

ناز   naz *n.*   blandishment, coquetry, grace

نازرک   nazurk *adj.*   delicate, subtle, abstruse

ناساز   nasaz *adj.*   indisposed, ill, adverse, discordant

ناسئی   nasəi *adj., n.*   unmindful, inattentive, negligent; unmindful person

ناکام   nakam *n., adj., adv.*   failure; unsuccessful, failed; unsuccessfully

ناکو   nako *n.*   uncle (father's or mother's brother); father-in-law

ناکوزاتک	nakozatk *n.*	cousin: uncle's son or daughter
ناگمان	nagwman *adj.*	unexpected, sudden
ناگه	nagə *adj.*	sudden, unexpected
نال	nal *n.*	horseshoe
نالائق	nalayq *adj., n.*	incapable, unworthy, unfit; unworthy person
نام	nam *n.*	name, designation, repute, fame
ناماور	namavər *adj.*	famous, named, renowned
نامدار	namdar *adj.*	famous, known, celebrated
نامزد	namzəd *adj.*	nominated
ناموز	namuz *n.*	honor, esteem, respect, reputation
نامی	nami *adj.*	famous, known, celebrated
نان	nan *n.*	bread, (piece of) bread
نانبائی	nanbai *n.*	baker
نانوائی	nanvai *n.*	baker
نان ونگن	nan-w-nəgən *n.*	bread-and-bread: food
ناوانده	navanda *adj., n.*	illiterate

ناوک navəkk *n.* arrowhead

ناوهش navəhš *adj.* angry, annoyed

ناہک nahəkk *adj., adv.* unjust, wrongful, illegal, false

ناہکہ nahəkka *adv.* unjustly, wrongfully, falsely

نائب nayb *n., adj.* deputy, regent, vice-

نائی nai *n.* barber

نپاد nypad *n.* bedding

نپت nəpt *n.* oil, petroleum

نپس nəpəs *n.* breath, life

نترس nəturs *adj.* fearless, dauntless, brave

نجات nyjat *n.* salvation

ندر nədr *n.* sacrifice (of an animal) offered at a shrine

نر nər *n.* man, male

نرخ nyrəx *n.* price, value

نرم nərm *adj.* soft, mild, tender, lenient

نرینگ nəriəg *n., adj.* male, man

نز nəzz *adj., adv.* near, nearby

نزام	**nyzam** *n.*	system, organization
نزانت	**nəzant** *adj.*	ignorant, foolish
نزانت‌کار	**nəzantkar** *n., adj.*	ignorant, inexperienced, naive
نزر	**nəzər** *n.*	eyesight; the evil eye
نزور	**nyzor** *adj.*	weak, debilitated, feeble
نزوری	**nyzori** *n.*	weakness
نزیخ	**nəzix** *adv., comp. prep.*	near, at, having
نزّیک	**nəzzik** *adj.*	near
نزّیخی	**nəzzixi** *n., adj.*	relative; close relative
نُسخان	**nwsxan** *n.*	loss, deficit, wastage
نسگ	**nəsəg** *v.*	to grind up, powder
نسیب	**nysib** *n.*	fortune, lot, destiny
نشان	**nyšan** *n.*	sign, indication, symptom
نشانگ	**nyšanəg** *n.*	target, mark
نشانگ جنگ	**nyšanəg jənəg** *v.*	to shoot at a target
نشانگ کنگ	**nyšanəg kənəg** *v.*	to aim at, make (something one's) target
نشک	**nəšk** *n.*	symptom, sign, indication, visible trace

نُصقان	nwṣqan *n.*	loss, damage, harm, wastage, injury
نصیب	nyṣib *n.*	fortune, fate, destiny
نصیبو	nyṣibo *n.*	fate, destiny, lot, fortune
نظام	nyẓam *n.*	system, organization
نظر	nəẓər *n.*	eyesight; evil eye
نعل	n'al *n.*	horseshoe
نغن	nəGən *n.*	party, feast, invitation, call
نفا	nəfa *n.*	profit, gain, benefit, advantage, interest
نفس	nəfəs *n.*	breath, life
نفع	nəf'a *n.*	profit, benefit, advantage, gain
نقشگ	nəqšəg *n.*	map, chart, sketch, scene, features, profile
نُقصان	nwqṣan *n.*	loss, damage, wastage, harm
نقلی	nəqli *adj.*	artificial, immitation
نکاح	nykaḥ *n.*	marriage, wedding
نکار	nykar *adj.*	setting aside, not taking part; surpassing, outstanding
نکان	nykan *n.*	foodstuffs, supplies, groceries
نکاه	nykah *n.*	wedding, marriage ceremony

نکسان nwksan *n.* loss, damage, harm, wastage

نگا داری nygadari *n.* supervision, surveillance, caring for

نگد nəgd *n., adj., adv.* cash, ready money, in cash

نگدی nəgdi *n.* cash, ready money

نگران nygran *adj.* sad, depressed

نگن nəgən *n.* bread

نماز nymaz *n.* Islamic ritual prayer

نماش nymaš *n.* Islamic ritual prayer

نمائیندگ nwmayndəg *n.* representative

نمب məmb *n., adj.* damp earth; damp

نمبر nəmbər *n.* number

نمشت nymyšt *n.* writing, script

نمشتانک nymyštank *n.* writing, essay, article

نمشتکار nymyštkar *n.* writer

نمشتگ nymyštəg *n.* writing

نمک حلالی nəmək ḥəlali *n.* faithfulness, loyalty

نمنّ nəmann *n.* refusal, denial, rejection

نمونه nəmuna *n.* sample, specimen, example, pattern, model

ننج	nynj *adj.*	pure
نندجاه	nyndjah *n.*	seat
نندگ	nyndəg *v.*	to sit, to stay, live (in a place)
نندغ	nyndəG *v.*	to sit, to stay, live
ننگ	nəng *n.*	honor
ننگ دار	nəngdar *n., adj.*	man of honor, honorable
ننگر	nəngər *adj.*	honorable
ننوات	nənvat *n.*	plea, entreaty, importunity
نوبت	nəwbət *n.*	time, turn, era
نوٹ	noT *n.*	(currency) note
نوخ	nox *adj.*	wonderful, marvellous, strange
نود	nəvəd *adj.*	ninety
نود و پنج	nəvəd-w-pənj *adj.*	ninety-five
نود و چار	nəvəd-w-car *adj.*	ninety-four
نود و سه	nəvəd-w-sə *adj.*	ninety-three
نود و شش	nəvəd-w-šəš *adj.*	ninety-six
نود و نو	nəvəd-w-nəw *adj.*	ninety-nine
نود و ہشت	nəvəd-w-həšt *adj.*	ninety-eight

نود و ہفت	nəvəd-w-həft *adj.*	ninety-seven
نود و یک	nəvəd-w-yək *adj.*	ninety-one
نودی	nodi *adj., adv.*	swift, quick; swiftly
نور	nur *n.*	light, illumination, brilliance
نوشتہ کنگ	nəvəšta kənəg *n.*	to write
نوشکے	noške *n.*	Noshki, a city in Pakistani Baluchistan
نوک	nok *adj.*	new
نوکر	nokər *n.*	servant, workman, employee
نوکری	nokəri *n.*	service, employment, job
نوک سر	nok-sər *n.*	new year
نوکی	noki *adv.*	presently, recently
نومبر	nəwmbər *n.*	November
نون	nun *adv.*	now, presently, at the present time
نونزدگ	nõzdəg *adj.*	nineteen
نویکلا	nəvekla *adj.*	novel, unique, new, strange
نویکلائی	nəveklai *n.*	individuality
نویں کار	nəvĩkar *n.*	invention, innovation, creation

نہ	nə *neg. adv.*	no, not
نُہ	nw *adj.*	nine
نہار	nəhar *n., adj.*	wild animal, beast; ferocious
نہال	nyhal *n.*	sprout, seedling
نہر	nəhr *n.*	price, value
نہمت	nəhmət *n.*	determination, resolution
نی	ni *adv.*	now
نے	nəy *conj.*	neither
نیابت	nyabət *n.*	sub-district, division of a district
نیاد	niad *n.*	price, value
نیاد	nyad *n.*	meeting, sitting
نیام	niyam *n.*	middle, center
نیامگی	niyamgi *n., adj.*	average, medium, middle
نیامی	niyami *n.*	broker, agent
نیّت	niyyət *n.*	intention, resolve
نیٹ	neT *adv.*	finally, after all, in the end
نیخی	nixi *n.*	prosperity, betterment, welfare

نیزگار	nezgar *n., adj.*	pauper, poor; poor person
نیست	nest *v.*	(there) is not, (there) are not
نیستی	nesti *n.*	poverty
نیک	nek *adj., n.*	good, virtuous, pious, pure, God-fearing
نیکاح	niykah *n.*	marriage, wedding
نیل	nil *adj., n.*	blue, indigo; indigo plant
نیلبو	nilbo *adj.*	bluish
نیلی	nili *adj.*	blue
نیم	nem *adj.*	half...and a half
نیمروچ	nemroc *n.*	noon
نیمروچا	nemroca *adv.*	at noon
نیمگ	neməg *n.*	half, half portion
نیمگ	neməg *n.*	direction, side
نِیمون	nimon *n.*	excuse, alibi, pretext
نِیں	ñi *adv.*	presently, now, at the present time
نِیوگ	nivəg *n.*	fruit

و

و	w *conj.*	and
وام	vaəm *conj.*	nevertheless, however, even though
واب	vab *n.*	sleep, dream
واپار	vapar *n.*	merchant, trader, businessman
واپاری	vapari *n.*	business, trade, commerce
واتر	vatər *adv.*	back, again, returning
واتری	vatri *n.*	return, reversion, retreat, arrival back
واجب	vajyb *adj.*	necessary, incumbent, obligatory, due
واجگ	vajəg *n., adj.*	sir, mister; almighty, masterly
واجەکار	vajəkar *n., adj.*	hero; heroic
واد	vad *n.*	salt
وادان	vadan *adj.*	prosperous
وادانی	vadani *n.*	prosperity
وار	var *n.*	time, occasion, turn

وار	var *n., adj.*	troubled, unfortunate, indigent, poor (person)
وارث	varyṣ *n.*	heir, owner; guardian
وارس	varys *n.*	heir, guardian
واری	vari *n.*	labor, effort; trouble, woe
واری	vari *n.*	turn, time
وازدار	vazdar *n.*	owner, master, proprieter, boss
واژه	važah *n.*	sir, gentleman
واژه	važa *adj.*	capturing, seizing, taking
واس	vas *n.*	kiss
واک	vak *n.*	power, control, authority
واک	vak *n.*	energy, power
واگ	vag *n.*	bridle
وال	val *n.*	yard
والیکم سلام	valekum səlam *interj.*	hello, and greetings to you (*lit.* And peace be upon you!)
وام	vam *n.*	loan, debt, credit, money borrowed
وانتجاه	vantjah *n.*	school, educational institution
واندا	vanda *adj.*	free, at leisure

واندائ	vandai *n.*	leave, leisure, free time
واندکائ	vandkai *n.*	leisure, free time, leave
وانگ / وانغ	vanəg/vanəG *v.*	to read, study
وانگڑ	vangəR *n.*	eggplant
وانگ و زانگ	vanəg-w-zanəg *n.*	reading-and-knowing: literacy, knowledge, education
وانوخ	vanox *n.*	reader
وانوک / وانوخ	vanok/vanox *n.*	(male) student
واه	vah *interj.*	bravo! well done!
واہد	vahəd *n.*	time
واہر	vahyr *n.*	help, aid, assistance
واه زاری	vahzari *n.*	screaming, weeping and crying
واہگ	vahəg *n.*	concern, regard, consideration, demand, requirement; goal, objective; love, affection
واہم	vahəm *conj.*	however, nevertheless, even though
وائے	vae *interj.*	alas! ouch!
وایگ	vayəg *n.*	concern, regard, consideration; demand, requirement; goal, objective; love, affection

وبا	vəba *n.*	epidemic
وپا دار	vəpadar *adj.*	faithful
وت	vət *prep.*	one (self)
وتاک	vətak *n.*	camp, temporary lodging
وتسر	vətsər *n., adj.*	absolute, all-powerful, dictatorial, sole
وتسرا	vətsəra *adv.*	independently, of one's own will, dictatorially, alone
وت مه وت	vət-mə-vət *adv.*	one another, each other, among (our, your, them) selves
وتن	vətən *n.*	homeland
وتواجئ	vət-vajəi *n.*	self-determination
وتن دُژمن	vətən dwžmən *n.*	traitor
وتی	vəti *adj.*	(one's) own
وٹّغ	vəTTəG *v.*	to spin, to weave
وَٹم	vəTym *n.*	deceit, delusion, guile
وحد	vəḥd *n.*	time
وحی	vəḥi *n.*	revelation
وخت	vəxt *n.*	time, period, age
وختی	vəxti *adv.*	on time

وختے	vəxtəy *adv.*	sometime
ودّ	vədd *n.*	addition, increase, augment, increment
ودار	vədar *n.*	waiting, expecting
ودّگ	vəddəg *v.*	to grow, increase
ودّہغ	vəddəhG *v.*	to extend, increase, grow, expand, thrive, proceed, advance
ودّھیک	vəddhik *adj.*	more, much, too much, too many
ودی	vədi *adj.*	born, found, appeared
وظیفا	vədifa *n.*	stipend, pension, scholarship; special prayer recited regularly as an individual, private act of worship
ودیگی	vədigi *n.*	birth
وڈّائی	vəDDai *n.*	pride, arrogance, haughtiness
وڈّہی	vəDDhi *n.*	bribe
وڈّہی وار	vəDDhi-var *adj.*	one who accepts bribe, corrupt
وردش	vərdəš *n.*	exercise (athletic or mental), exertion
وردن	vərdyn *n.*	food, edibles
ورَغ	verəG *v.*	to cut

وَرَغ	vərəG *n.*	embezzlement, fraud, misappropriation
ورگ	vərəg *v.*	to eat, drink
ورنا	vərna *n.*	slave, bondsman
ورنا	vərna *n.*	youth, young man, young
ورنائ	vərnai *n.*	youth, adolescence
ور و وردن	vər-w-vərdyn *n.*	eating-and-food: food and drink
وړ	vəR *n.*	kind, sort, type, category, way, method
وړدن	vəRdən *n.*	foodstuffs, food, diet
وړ وړ	vəR-vəR *adj.*	various kinds
وزّت	vəzzət *n.*	worry, concern
وزن	vəzən *n.*	weight
وزیر	vəzir *n.*	(cabinet) minister
وزیری	vəziri *n., adj.*	cabinet, ministerial
وسّ	vəss *n.*	control, grasp, hold
وسرک	vəsyrk *n.*	father-in-law
وسپگ	vəspəg *v.*	to sleep
وسم	vəsəm *n.*	village

وسّو	vəssu *n.*	mother-in-law
وسواس	vəsvas *n.*	doubt, uncertainty, suspicion
وسّی	vəssi *n.*	mother-in-law
وسیله	vəsila *n.*	source, means, way, connection, medium
وشّ / وہشّ	vəšš / vəhšš *adj.*	happy, glad, fine; sweet
وشّ	vəšš *adj.*	sweet
وش آحت	vəšaḥət *n.*	welcome, reception
وشّال	vəššal *adj.*	happy, glad
وشاہت	vəššaht *n.*	welcome
وشحال	vəššḥal *adj.*	glad, hapy
وشّبو	vəššbo *n., adj.*	perfume; perfumed
وشّی	vəšši *n.*	happiness, joy, rejoicing
وضو	vwẕu *n.*	ablutions necessary before Islamic prayers
وطن	vəṭən *n.*	homeland
وطن دُژمن	vəṭən dwžmən *n., adj.*	traitor, renegade
وظیفہ	vəẓifa *n.*	special prayer recited regularly as a private act of worship; stipend, pension, scholarship

وعظ	v'əẓ *n.*	sermon, religious oration
وفا	vəfa *n.*	faithfulness, fidelity, fulfillment of a promise
وفات	vəfat *n.*	death
وقت	vəqt *n.*	time
وقتی	vəqti *adv.*	on time
وقف	vəqf *n.*	devotion, dedication, a bequest or endowment or trust made for pious purposes
وکت	vəkt *n.*	time
وکتی	vəkti *n.*	on time
وکشی	vəkši *adj., n.*	wild, barbarous, brutal, ferocious, madman, wild beast
وکیل	vəkil *n.*	lawyer, advocate, pleader, attorney
وکیلی‌کار	vəkili-kar *n.*	delegation, representation, agency
ولّ	vəll *n.*	vine
ولائت	vylayət *n.*	country, state, realm, land
ولی	vəli *n.*	saint
ولے	vəle *conj.*	but

ولیکن vəlekyn *conj.* but, nevertheless, evenso

ونّا vənna *n.* bridegroom

ونتکار vəntkar *adj.* educated, literate

ونتکاری vəntkari *n.* education

ونڈ vənD *n.* instalment; (equal) part, portion, section

واد / وہاذ vad/vəhaz *n.* salt

وہار vəhar *n., adj.* unfavorably known, notorious

وہاری vəhari *n.* notoriety

وہد vəhd *n.* time

وہدی vəhdi *adv.* interim, temporary

وہڑد vəhRd *n.* foodstuffs, food, diet

وہم vəhem *n.* suspicion

وہم vəhm *n.* doubt, suspicion

وی vəi *n.* age (of a person)

ویر vir *n.* greed, avarice

ویران veran *adj.* deserted, desolate

ویرانداں verandã *adj.* deserted, desolate, laid waste, barren

ولیس	vəysah *n.*	confidence, trust, reliance
وِیل	vəyl *n.*	difficulty, trouble, catastrophe, calamity
وِیلُم	veylwm *n.*	time, period, age

ه

حاتر	hatyr *n.*	heart
حاتون	hatun *n.*	lady *(honorific)*
حاٹی	haTi *n.*	strength, power, energy, ability, force
حاجی	haji *n.*	pilgrim (person who makes the Islamic pilgrimage to Mecca)
حاخ	hax *n.*	ashes
حاڈال	haDal *n.*	skeleton
حار	har *n.*	flood
حاروس	haros *n.*	marriage, wedding
حاری	hari *adj.*	flood, flooding
حازر	hazyr *adj.*	present, at hand, in attendance
حاک	hak *n.*	dirt, earth, soil, dust
حاکم	hakym *n., adj.*	governor, ruler; ruling, royal
حاکوت	hakot *n.*	earth-pile, heap of dirt
حال	hal *n.*	state, condition, news, information

هالتاک	haltak *n.*	newspaper
هامغ	haməG *adj.*	raw, unripe, uncooked, immature, temporary
هامگ	haməg *adj.*	raw, unripe, uncooked, immature, temporary
هامون	hamun *n.*	lake
هامین	hamen *n.*	August, the harvest season
هاں	hã *interj.*	yes
هان	han *n., adj.*	king, khan, lord; lordly, kingly
هاو	haw *interj.*	yes
هاور	hawr *n.*	rain
هاے	hae *interj.*	woe! alas!
هبدگ	həbdəg *adj.*	seventeen
هبر	həbər *n.*	word, matter, news, talk, thing
هبرتاک	həbərtak *n.*	newspaper
هبر وهال	həbər-w-hal *n.*	news-and-condition: news, information
هپت	həpt *adj.*	seven
هپتاد ونو	həptadonəw *adj.*	sixty-nine
هپتگ	həptəg *n.*	week; Saturday

ہپتمی	həptəmi *adj.*	seventh
ہپدہ	həpda *adj.*	seventeen
ہتھیار	həthyar *n.*	weapon, arms
ہٹ	həT *n.*	shop, store
ہجّ	həjj *n.*	Hajj (the Islamic pilgrimage)
ہجّل	həjjəl *n.*	pause, delay, interval, intermission
ہدّ	hədd *n.*	border, boundary line, place
ہدیس	hədis *n.*	narration; tradition relating to sayings and deeds of the Prophet Muhammad
ہدیگ	hədyəg *n.*	present, gift
ہڈّ	həDD *n.*	bone
ہڈّ	həDD *pred. adj.*	standing, erected, built; stopping, waiting
ہذ	hyẓ *n.*	hesitation, vascillation, wavering
ہر	hər *n.*	donkey
ہر	hər *adj.*	each, every
ہراب	hərab *adj.*	bad, out of order, broken, of poor quality
ہرچ	hərc *n.*	costs, expenses, spending

ہر چُنت	hər-cwnt *conj.*	although, though, even though, even if, however much
ہر دل دوست	hərdyl dost *adj.*	popular, one liked by all
ہرگز	hərgyz *adv.*	absolutely, definitely *(usually in negative phrases)*
ہڑ دُڑ	həR-dwR *n.*	commotion, rioting
ہڑس	hyRs *n.*	greed
ہزار	həzar *adj., n.*	thousand
ہزاری	həzari *adj.*	of a thousand, worth a thousand (rupees, etc.)
ہژدہ	həžda *adj.*	eighteen
ہژّار	hwžžar *adj.*	clever, smart, intelligent
ہژیاری	hwžyari *n.*	intelligence, cleverness, alertness, awareness
ہستی	həsti *n.*	life, being, existence; great person
ہشت	həšt *adj.*	eight
ہشتاد	həštad *adj.*	eighty
ہشتاد و پنج	həštad-w-pənj *adj.*	eighty-five
ہشتاد و دو	həštad-w-do *adj.*	eighty-two
ہشتاد و سہ	həštad-w-səh *adj.*	eighty-three

هشتادوشش	həštad-w-šəš *adj.*	eighty-six
هشتادوهشت	həštad-w-həšt *adj.*	eighty-eight
هشتمی	həštəmi *adj.*	eighth
هفت	həft *adj.*	seven
هفتاد	həftad *adj.*	seventy
هفتادوچار	həftad-w-car *adj.*	seventy-four
هفتاد ودو	həftad-w-do *adj.*	seventy-two
هفتادوسه	həftad-w-səh *adj.*	seventy-three
هفتادوشش	həftad-w-šəš *adj.*	seventy-six
هفتادونو	həftad-w-nəw *adj.*	seventy-nine
هفتادوهفت	həftad-w-həft *adj.*	seventy-seven
هفتادویک	həftad-w-yək *adj.*	seventy-one
هفتگ	həftəg *n.*	week
هک	həkk *n., adj.*	right, due; true, real, genuine
هکّا	həkka *adj.*	stunned
هل بل	həl-bəl *n.*	movement, disturbance
هُلجا	hwlja *n.*	noise, uproar, commotion
هلک	həlk *n.*	village

ہلّگ	həlləg *v.*	to stop, finish, end
ہلمہ	həlma *n.*	attack, assault
ہلہ	hələ *n., interj.*	hurry, commotion, tumult; hurry up!
ہم	həm *part.*	also, too
ہما	hwma *demon.*	that, those *(emphatic)*; he, she, it, they *(emphatic)*
ہماساہگ	həmasahəg *n., adj.*	neighbor, neighboring
ہمباز	həmbaz *n.*	embrace
ہمبازگ	həmbazəg *v.*	to embrace, welcome
ہمبل	həmbəl *n.*	fellow
ہمبو	həmbo *n., adj.*	fragrance, perfume; fragrant, perfumed
ہمّت	hymmət *n.*	power, strength, ability, capability, capacity
ہم دپ	həmdəp *pred. adj.*	favorable, suitable; similar
ہم دل	həmdyl *n., adj.*	friend, friendly, sympathetic
ہمراہ	həmrah *n., adj.*	companion, fellow traveller
ہمراہی	həmrahi *n.*	companionship, company
ہمزُبان	həmzwban *n.*	confere, confidant (*Lit.* "same-language")

ہمسایُغ	həmsayəG *n.*	neighbor
ہمسری	həmsəri *n.*	equality, equivalence; friendship (between two equals)
ہمسلہ	həmsələ *adj.*	united, agreed, having the same opinion, purpose or plan
ہم سنگ	həmsəng *n.*	equal, level, on a par
ہمک	həmwk *adj.*	different, various, dissimilar, diverse
ہم گونگ	həmgonəg *n.*	resemblance, resembling, similarity
ہم گیر	həmgir *n.*	overwhelming, overrunning (from all sides)
ہمود	həmud *adv.*	right there
ہموش وار	həmošvar *pred. adj.*	accustomed, habituated
ہنجرو	hynjro *n.*	trap, cage
ہند	hənd *n.*	house, residential building
ہند	hənd *n.*	place, area, region
ہندگ	həndəg *v.*	to laugh
ہنر	hwnər *n.*	art, skill, craftsmanship, virtue, merit
ہنروند	honərvənd *n.*	craftsman

هنروندی	honərvəndi *n.*	craftsmanship
هو	həw *interj.*	yes
هوار / اوار	həvar/əvar *pred. adj.*	shared, in common, joint
هوپ	hop *n.*	epidemic
هوَر	həvər *n.*	rain
هوس	həvəs *n.*	lust, greed
هوش	hoš *n.*	senses, consciousness
هوش مند	hošmənd *adj.*	sensible, intelligent, prudent
هوف	hof *n.*	epidemic, plague
هیذ	heyẓ *n.*	extract, essence
هیرا	hira *n.*	diamond
هیگ	həyg *n.*	egg
هیل	həyl *n.*	habit
هیلاک	həylak *pred. adj.*	habituated, accustomed, addicted

ے

یا	ya *conj.*	or
یات	yat *n.*	memory, recollection
یات گیری	yatgiri *n., adj.*	memorial, memory
یا داشت	yaddašt *n.*	memory, recollection
یار	yar *n.*	beloved, dear friend
یاری	yari *n.*	friendship
یا زده	yazda *adj.*	eleven
یاغی	yaGi *n., adj.*	traitor, renegade
یاغی گری	yaGi gəri *n.*	treason, treachery
یاگی	yagi *n., adj.*	rebel, rebellious
یال	yal *pred. adj.*	thought, opinion
یا نزدگ	yãzdəg *adj.*	eleven
یکجا	yəjja *pred. adj.*	united, unified, joint
یخ	yəxx *n., adj.*	cold
یزدان	yəzdan *n.*	God

یک	yək *adj.*	one, a, an
یکجا	yəkja *adv.*	together, at the same time, a the same place
یک دار	yəkdar *n.*	boat
یک دمان	yək-dəman *adj., adv.*	sudden, unexpected; suddenly unexpectedly
یکره	yəkrəh *adj.*	straightforward, candid
یکسر	yəksər *adj.*	alone, lonely
یکشنبه	yəkšəmbe *n.*	Sunday
یکه	yəkh *pred. adj.*	united, unified, joint
یکی	yəkki *n.*	agreement, unity, concord
یکیکی	yəkyəki *adj.*	individual
یکیتی	yəkəyyẽ *adj.*	only, single
یقینی	yəqini *adv.*	absolutely, certainly, definitely
یل	yəl *adj.*	pretty, beautiful, handsome; strong, stout, vigorous
یلو	yəlo *n., adj.*	vagabond, wanderer; wandering, roving
یله	yələ *adj.*	free, astray, loose, leaving
یلئی	yələi *adj.*	free, loose, astray, at liberty